FROM
BICYCLE
TO
BENTLEY
A BOOKMAKER'S STORY

I dedicate this book to jockey-turned-bookmaker Vic Gardner, who encouraged me in my early days and presented the first opportunity to kick-start my bookmaking career at Bristol dogs, to Keith Higgs who elevated me to the rails, and to bookmaker Eddie Baxter (Avalon Turf) who also encouraged my interest in bookmaker politics.

Thanks

Firstly I thank my sister Liz for helping with photographs, and secondly I thank two Old Harrovian baronets, Sir Mark Prescott and Sir Rupert Mackeson, both well-known either side of the Irish Sea in racing and coursing circles. Sir Mark kindly wrote the foreword while Sir Rupert has acted as my editor from the day last year when he urged me to write this at Salisbury racecourse. Also thanks to Jim Beavis for reading the draft and passing it fit for publication. Finally thanks to Charles Hewitt of Pen and Sword books and his lovely staff who have been so cheerfully helpful to my editor and myself in getting the book out so quickly after receiving the typescript.

FROM BICYCLE TO BENTLEY

A BOOKMAKER'S STORY

Stephen Little

WHITE OWL

AN IMPRINT OF PEN & SWORD BOOKS LTD.
YORKSHIRE – PHILADELPHIA

First published in Great Britain in 2023 and reprinted in 2024 by
PEN AND SWORD WHITE OWL
An imprint of
Pen & Sword Books Ltd
Yorkshire – Philadelphia

Copyright © Stephen Little, 2023, 2024

ISBN 978 1 03610 193 0

The right of Stephen Little to be identified as Author of this work has been asserted by him in accordance with the Copyright, Designs and Patents Act 1988.

A CIP catalogue record for this book is available from the British Library.

All rights reserved. No part of this book may be reproduced or transmitted in any form or by any means, electronic or mechanical including photocopying, recording or by any information storage and retrieval system, without permission from the Publisher in writing.

Typeset in Times New Roman 12/16 by
SJmagic DESIGN SERVICES, India.
Printed and bound in the UK by CPI Group (UK) Ltd, Croydon, CR0 4YY.

Pen & Sword Books Limited incorporates the imprints of Atlas, Archaeology, Aviation, Discovery, Family History, Fiction, History, Maritime, Military, Military Classics, Politics, Select, Transport, True Crime, Air World, Frontline Publishing, Leo Cooper, Remember When, Seaforth Publishing, The Praetorian Press, Wharncliffe Local History, Wharncliffe Transport, Wharncliffe True Crime, White Owl and After the Battle.

For a complete list of Pen & Sword titles please contact

PEN & SWORD BOOKS LIMITED
George House, Units 12 & 13, Beevor Street, Off Pontefract Road,
Barnsley, South Yorkshire, S71 1HN, England
E-mail: enquiries@pen-and-sword.co.uk
Website: www.pen-and-sword.co.uk

or
PEN AND SWORD BOOKS
1950 Lawrence Rd, Havertown, PA 19083, USA
E-mail: uspen-and-sword@casematepublishers.com
Website: www.penandswordbooks.com

Contents

Foreword by Sir Mark Prescott, Bt vii

Chapter 1	Early days and schools, and first race meeting 1
Chapter 2	Gap year on a budget.. 10
Chapter 3	Gap year continues.. 15
Chapter 4	First job and first coursing meeting...................................... 21
Chapter 5	Back on the road, first racecourse job, every course on a bike and photofinish betting............................ 25
Chapter 6	Apprenticeship, on the dole, first licence and pitches.......... 32
Chapter 7	In at the deep end and early policy decisions...................... 39
Chapter 8	Getting known and rule 4 45
Chapter 9	Cyril Stein, other leading bookmakers, and keeping warm 50
Chapter 10	Owning horses and dogs, night in a police cell, breathalysed, and backgammon 56
Chapter 11	Computers and mobile phones... 64
Chapter 12	Increasing turnover and a new Bentley................................ 70
Chapter 13	Another house move, more large bets and a suspect race.. 76

Chapter 14	Bookmaking politics and the threat to the betting ring	82
Chapter 15	They know not what they do	88
Chapter 16	Notice to quit and joining Corals	93
Chapter 17	Redundancy and retirement to stud	98
Chapter 18	Looking back	103

Coursing Appendix	110
Betting Appendix	117
Clerking before computers	120

Foreword

I don't suppose there will ever be another Stephen Little. The days of the independent bookmaker have long gone, and it is my privilege, therefore, to be asked to write this brief foreword to the entertaining memories of a fascinating man, whom I have known for over 50 years.

The son of a Lincolnshire vicar, when aged only 12, and at prep school, he made his first book on the Lincoln Handicap. On leaving Uppingham, he went coursing for the first time at North Herts in 1965, and obtained his first bookmakers' licence in 1971. Later that year he stood up at the Waterloo Cup for the first time.

Famous for having attended every race course in Britain on his bicycle, the same could probably be said of every coursing meeting in the land, and it was at an autumn meeting of the small Mid Essex Coursing Club, where today lorries thunder along the M11 motorway, 10 miles south of Newmarket, that I first met him.

It had been an excellent morning. Still, calm and mellow, the hares had run well on the dry chalky land, flicking up puffs of soil as they ran straight up the rolling fields, and disappeared from view over the next rise, with only the mounted judge able to see what work took place after the first turn.

"Ideal coursing" commented the judge to the coursing correspondent, John McCririck, on his return from a lengthy course completed out of view of the crowd, "you'll have to rely entirely on me for every single course description!"

From Bicycle to Bentley, A Bookmaker's Story

In those days Annie Bazeley, the stalwart South Eastern representative of the British Field Sports Society was relentless in checking that everyone on a coursing field was a member of that organisation. At the same time, she also secured contributions to the inevitable club raffle and the beaters fund.

At the lunch break, Annie Bazeley cornered John McCririck, Crispin Dennis & Stephen Little, who had all taken refuge in the autumn sunshine on top of a straw rick. Cheered on by the beaters below, who were munching their packed lunches, Annie's outstretched hands clasped contributions from the two first named, but Stephen's pound note, on the stillest of days, fluttered close to her fingertips, only to swoop back, guided by some unseen deity, back into his bookmaker's bag. Good natured jeers and derision from all around accompanied the scene.

There was another glimpse into the future at The Koni Barbican Cup, run by East of England Coursing Club and sponsored by land owner Bill Banks. The Barbican was second only to the Waterloo Cup in its importance in the coursing Calander. For 64 dogs it took place on vast fens near Peterborough on a specially prepared field. The great and the good watched from a decommissioned London Bus. On the opening day, Stephen arrived on his bicycle and, still unknown to many, promptly stood up on a pink plastic milk crate and called out in a gentle voice "I'll take 6/4 each of two".

An enormous punter from the travelling community, unwound himself from a fogged up white Mercedes, clutching a roll of bank notes and declaring to a group of onlookers, anxious for this young bookmaker's welfare, that he'd be "delighted to take a bit of that".

Three years later the scene was repeated, the only difference being that Stephen was in a Rolls Royce and the traveller was in the same Mercedes.

From the youth hostels of his cycling days, he graduated via the cauldron of the betting ring at Cheltenham, to one of the few privately owned houses in the Royal Crescent at Bath. This fascinating book with no frills, fancies or exaggerations tells you how.

Foreword

Always his own man, devoid of pretentiousness, unfailingly logical and utterly dependable, these pages are a joy to read and are an important record of the times. Moreover, it shows how it is possible to get to the very top of a chosen profession, without knowingly causing harm to anyone along the way.

M.P.
28.06.23

Chapter 1

Early days and schools, and first race meeting

I am often asked what the largest bet I ever took was. There are three possible answers: the largest stake, the largest liability, or the largest take-out, i.e. potential return of winnings plus stake, which is the true measure of the size of a bet.

The largest stake was £150,000 to win £75,000 *(2023 equivalent £280,500 to win £140,250)* on Double Trigger in the Ascot Gold Cup in June 1996; to put the bet in perspective, the punter who had the bet was still in front on the week after it ran second to Classic Cliché. The bet with the largest liability was £250,000-30,000 *(£492,500-59,100)* Gimme Five, in one of the handicap hurdles at Cheltenham Festival in March 1994; it was difficult to hedge it properly as it started as 4/1 favourite, and though it finished well down the field to Tindari it was still an uncomfortable race to watch. But the real largest bet, with a take-out of £330,000 *(£617,100)*, was £210,000-120,000 *(£392,700-224,400)* Sound Man, which finished third at 11/8 to Klairon Davis in the Champion Chase at Cheltenham in 1996.[1]

These bets all lost, but there were plenty of six-figure winning bets as well. I am still trying to forget Fujiyama Crest, Frankie Dettori's seventh winner of seven at Ascot in 1996; that was one of those 'I was there and I wish I hadn't been' days, as were two consecutive disastrous days at Cheltenham a few years previously. More about these and other mishaps in a later chapter.

---

1. 2023 values calculated from the Bank of England inflation calculator.

From Bicycle to Bentley, A Bookmaker's Story

What follows is a tale of slow progress from starting with next to nothing, except ambition and determination to follow my vocation of bookmaking, graduating from pedalling to the races on a bicycle to driving there in a Bentley, and finishing with more than nothing – ambition achieved!

During the war, my father had served in the RAF as a chaplain; his brother was a bomber pilot, posthumously awarded a DFC after his Stirling bomber was shot down near Berlin on his last scheduled raid. After my father left the RAF, in 1946 my parents and elder brother, David, were living with my mother's parents in Mill Hill in North London. I was born during this time in a West Hampstead nursing home, and the family moved to Nottingham a year later when my father was appointed to his first parish at St Ann's, one of the rougher areas of that city.

I don't remember much about my early life in Nottingham. The vicarage was in Woodborough Road where it meets Robin Hood Chase; the church was at the southern end of Robin Hood Chase on St Ann's Well Road. Both church and vicarage were demolished many years ago. From the age of 5 I attended Waverley School, a small private school not far from home near Mansfield Road, where I remember being very proud when I was promoted one class up in mid-term.

The few things I do recall give a flavour of the times. There were trams in Woodborough Road. There were bomb sites all over Nottingham. I used to help count the church collections; they often included farthings (£1/960, or 0.104p), which were current then. You couldn't get anything for a single farthing, but there was a shop halfway down the Chase where you could get a glass of Tizer or dandelion & burdock for a halfpenny. A few doors down Woodborough Road was a post office where I opened my first savings account, and where I bought sweets on the day in February 1953 that they came off ration. My brother and I thought it was great that, wow, at last we didn't need any coupons to stock up on fruit gums and Mars Bars!

Unfortunately, we still needed to have money to buy them, which was also on ration as far as we were concerned. In the summer of 1951 on one of many visits to my grandparents in London, we went to the Festival of Britain.[2] When the Millennium Bridge over the Thames was first opened, there were many complaints about its apparent instability and unsettling motion, which reminded me of the Cakewalk at the Festival, a rickety tree-height walk that people actually paid to experience!

Our next move in 1953, shortly after my sister Elizabeth, aka Lizzie, was born, was to Skellingthorpe, a village five miles south-west of Lincoln where the skyline was dominated by the view of Lincoln Cathedral, set high in the upper part of the city. The parish was a combination of three parishes: the large village of Skellingthorpe, a dormitory for Lincoln; Doddington, a small village nearby that contains Doddington Hall, a large Elizabethan mansion; and Swallowbeck, a suburb at the southern end of Lincoln City. It was said to be the third largest parish in England by area at the time, before the more frequent combining of parishes. At first Swallowbeck had no church but only a corrugated iron church hall, but my father eventually oversaw the building of a new church there.

My father was appointed as chaplain to the judges when the assizes came to Lincoln. He said that his job was to say 'Amen' if a judge sentenced someone to be hanged, donned his black cap and said 'May God have mercy on your soul', but I don't think he was ever called upon to perform that duty. Part of the village of Skellingthorpe, with a very smelly abattoir, was known as Jerusalem, but the designation of Vicar of Jerusalem, though accurate, might have been a bit misleading.

---

2. The Festival of Britain was an event staged on the South Bank in London designed to encourage a feeling of recovery from the war and mark the centenary of the Great Exhibition. The 27-acre site contained exhibitions on various themes, with a fun-fair nearby, and related exhibitions throughout the country.

The vicarage was a large Victorian house set in nine acres of grounds, including some woodland, and a separate coach house with a hay loft. There was a long drive from the road bordered by rows of lime trees, with a paddock either side. This may sound rather grand, until I mention the rain that came through the large window overlooking the staircase, the crumbling plaster that regularly had to be scraped out of the bath, and the large growth of fungus high up on one wall of the dining room as a result of wet rot. There was no form of central heating, and many a morning I would wake up unable to see out of the windows because they were completely frosted over – but I could see my breath in the cold air. Behind the house was an apple orchard, with an old railway guard's van plonked in the middle. It was December when we moved in, and many of the outhouses were crammed full of rotting apples – the smell of them persisted for a very long time. Eventually, after a long campaign by my father, during which he sent a large specimen of the fungus to the Church Commissioners, a new vicarage was built for us beside the drive in one of the paddocks. Later, the old vicarage was sold and split into flats, and several new houses were built in the old grounds.

Most ginger cats are male, but we had a ginger cat named The Guddle who was a rarity in being female. She had litter after litter of kittens, and we enjoyed seeing them all grow up until they had to be given away. I have never lost my fondness for cats, and now always have a few, currently five, at home, but my first equine encounter was less auspicious. One of the paddocks was rented to two local girls who would keep a pony or two in it. I once got up on one of the ponies, but it subsequently bit my arm, and ever since I have been reluctant to get too close to a horse.

I never grew to like Lincoln. Three things typified the city for me: the football team slid from the second division to the fourth in successive seasons; the racecourse, managed by the Council, was allowed to decline and closed in the 1960s, though it remains largely intact; and when the Council was thinking about a theme for road names on a new housing estate, hands were thrown up in alarm when someone suggested using Derby winners, which would have been an association with gambling, shock, horror!

On moving to Skellingthorpe I attended the village Church of England school for two years, and at the age of 9 I was sent to the Dolphin School, a boys' boarding school in a large eighteenth-century house in extensive grounds near Newark. Founded by Rhodes Scholar Charles Roach, it closed in 1968 to become a private residence, now Grade II* listed. Sometimes we would attend the meet of the local hunt, and the headmaster, Charles' son Peter Roach, always drummed into us that we should be very careful about standing behind any horse. Excellent advice of course, but it did increase my wish to admire horses only from a distance.

One term I was bet that I would not use any swear words during the whole term. I didn't find this unduly difficult, but I had to be careful not to get caught out. For instance, on Sundays we attended services at the local church, All Saints in Winthorpe, which was unusual in being built of brick and having a hand carousel to allow all its six bells to be rung by a single person. It was also quite High Church, and instead of the congregation reciting the Nicene creed as is more common in Anglican services, we recited the longer Apostles' creed, which contains the phrase 'he descended into h**l'. The boys next to me were therefore checking that I briefly fell silent at that point.

My first venture into the world of bookmaking occurred at this school. It had been the custom for one of the boys to take bets on the Grand National each year, but during my last year there, someone else had claimed that position. I and two other boys decided to take bets on the Lincolnshire Handicap. This race and the Grand National were normally run on the Wednesday and Saturday respectively of the same week and formed the Spring Double, a popular ante-post bet in years gone by. We were not allowed to have money at the Dolphin School, so we had to bet in sweets, but although winner Marshal Pil was one of the favourites, my two partners and I had a good feed afterwards! By the time I was bookmaking, Lincoln had long closed, the Lincolnshire Handicap had moved to Doncaster 35 miles away in Yorkshire, and the notion of the Spring Double had faded.

Headmaster Peter Roach was a keen sportsman, especially for rugby, cricket and Nottingham Forest football. He was ecstatic when Forest won the FA Cup – he had even hired a special projector TV so that the whole school could watch the final. I was at the other end of the athletic spectrum, and conspired to be 'off games' whenever possible, so he was not impressed with me, though I surprised him by being one of few who did not succumb to any of the waves of illness that occasionally swept through the school. He warmed to me when I started to shine academically – I once got 147 out of 150 in a Latin exam, because I failed to realise that one word was a name that didn't need translating, and the number 147 still haunts me to this day – and he was completely won round when I brought some glory to the school by winning a scholarship to Uppingham.

And so to Uppingham, in Rutland, in September 1959, where at 13 years and 12 days I was the youngest boy in the school in my first term. My attendance there was made possible because the scholarship was augmented by an allowance for pupils who needed financial assistance, another for scholars who needed financial assistance, another for sons of clergy, and another for sons of clergy who needed assistance. Although my scholarship had been based on Classics (languages not horseraces!), it was decided that I should switch to mathematics and sciences, so I took Latin and Greek O levels early in my second year at the age of 14 before changing to what were known as B-side subjects for those O levels the following summer. I found Greek harder to master than Latin, mainly because of the different alphabet and more complicated word endings of the Attic version. I believe I may have been the only bookie of my time with an O level in Greek, unless there was a Greek bookie somewhere who had bothered to sit the exam.

Early days and schools, and first race meeting

It was during my first year at Uppingham that I became interested in racing. At that time I wasn't aware of any family connection to racing, but I later learned that my grandfather's cousin Wilfred Crawford was a trainer near Edinburgh, and his daughter Susan one of the world's leading equine artists whose best-known work is We Three Kings, head portraits of Arkle, Red Rum and Desert Orchid. We also have a photograph of my great-great-grandfather James Crawford acting as judge at Calcutta racecourse.

The opportunity to attend a race meeting at last came shortly before the start of my second year in September 1960 when I cycled the five miles from home to an ordinary meeting at Lincoln. Although I went into the cheapest course enclosure, opposite the main enclosure, I was captivated by the colours of the jockeys' silks, the line of bookmakers and the general atmosphere. In subsequent school holidays I would go further afield, to nearby courses such as Southwell, Market Rasen, Doncaster and Nottingham. York was too far for a return ride in one day, so when I went there for the Ebor meeting in August 1962 I joined the Youth Hostel Association and stayed in their York hostel. The meeting was extended that year to four days by the addition of the Variety Club charity meeting, and the overall experience of four top-class days of racing coupled with staying nearby and looking round the city was well worth the ride.

Although I became known as the school bookmaker, this was only a sporadic activity. Before being demoted to a Saturday, the Derby was run on a Wednesday during a lesson, so one boy would have a small radio in his pocket and an earpiece cable up his sleeve so that he could listen in and pass round the result to those who were interested. One year I took bets on the sports day 220 yards race. Someone had 10/- (50p) on the odds-on favourite, which I thought at the time was a big liability, but I thought another boy, in the same house as me, could beat him. The race was close between the two, but alas, there was no photo-finish and the favourite was adjudged the winner, contrary to my view, so not for the last time I had to grit my teeth and pay up with a smile – or was it a grimace? Another time I took bets on the annual election by the senior boys for Captain of Games. The favourite was a very good games player, but I considered he wasn't particularly popular. He was beaten by just one vote, so it was just as well that I had cast my vote appropriately.

Bicycles weren't generally allowed at Uppingham, but there were a few exceptions. One was for members of the History Society so that they could visit local sites of interest. I was tasked with going to Essendine Castle near Stamford to write a piece on it, but when I got there, there was not a stone of it left. Another exception was for boys who took up shooting, as the rifle range was a few miles from the town. Nowadays 'elf & safety would surely preclude boys cycling on a main road, the A47, with a .303 rifle slung over their backs, though of course ammunition was dispensed only under strict control once we got there. But shooting not only got me out of playing cricket but also resulted in my being allowed a bike at school. Thus I was able to go to the occasional nearby point-to-point and even a Leicester race meeting. Thousands of schoolchildren cycle to school, but not many have a journey of fifty miles to do so, but this was usually the most convenient way of transporting the bike at the beginning and end of term.

After O levels, I was set to take A levels in Maths, Higher Maths and Physics, but I had no thoughts about what career to follow until I gradually started to think I might like to be involved in racing. Had I been good at English I might have aimed at racing journalism, but as maths was my best subject I wanted to become a bookmaker. Not only the masters but also many of the boys said I was crazy not to go to university and go on from there, especially when I won the annual Constable Mathematics prize in my last term. But I thought – and still think now – that I was lucky to have something that I was sufficiently interested in to make a career of. The careers master, who had probably been at the school since it was founded in 1584, said he had never known anyone choose such a career. I was not alone

Early days and schools, and first race meeting

in making an unusual choice, as one of my contemporaries said he wanted to be a lion-tamer, and did indeed do so for a while.

Parents and teachers did their best to dissuade me from this path, but wisely did not attempt to force me to do something else against my will. I thought it prudent to continue with the two-year A level course in case I had second thoughts, but was relieved of the pressure to do well in them. Students of most subjects have masses of dates or vocabulary or formulae to learn, whatever flair they have for their subject, but this doesn't apply so much for maths. Thus my last few terms were fairly relaxed and I became quite proficient at croquet on the housemaster's lawn, because while other boys were swotting hard for exams, I had more time to get to know all the slopes and hollows of the lawn.

The law would not allow me to work in the betting industry before I was 18, so that was an excellent excuse to have a gap year (and a quarter), which I would make full use of by going racing. Back then, external exams were taken towards the end of July, rather than in May and June as now, so I duly sat my A levels, with extra papers for now-obsolete S levels, and left Uppingham by bicycle at the age of 16 on Friday, 26 July 1963 with a route mapped to take in Newbury, Lewes, Goodwood, Epsom, Yarmouth and Newmarket before eventually getting back to Skellingthorpe on 10 August, more than 800 miles of pedalling later. Freedom!!

Chapter 2

Gap year on a budget

The youth hostel at Streatley-on-Thames was to be my resting place for the first night. As I made progress south, passing the point where the Great Train Robbery would take place a few days later, the enormity of the changes to my life gradually dawned on me. I had been reasonably happy at Uppingham, but there were three aspects that I did not like: compulsory rugger, compulsory CCF (military training) and absence of girls. All three changed within a few years of my leaving. But now, no longer a schoolboy, at last I was able to go to meetings I had been able only to read about at school. I would make my first visit to Newbury the next day on the first day of the rest of my life. I had about fifteen months in front of me during which I was free to tour the country's racecourses at leisure. There were then about a dozen more racecourses than today and I planned my route over the rest of the time to visit as many as possible. Buckfastleigh had recently closed and I never made it to Rothbury, which had only one day's racing a year, nor Woore, before they also closed.

After Newbury it was on via Lewes to Goodwood, which at that time raced only four times a year, on the Tuesday to Friday at the end of July. A feature of Goodwood was, and still is, that there are no man-made buildings visible from the front of the grandstands, a contributory factor to its soubriquet of Glorious Goodwood. I recall that it was particularly hot that week, which, combined with the hills in the short distance between the racecourse and the youth hostel in East Marden where I stayed, made for uncomfortable cycling. The meeting's main race, the Sussex Stakes, was won by Queens Hussar, sire of Brigadier Gerard who won seventeen of his eighteen races, being beaten only at York at odds-on when I was betting in the Silver Ring and unfortunately missed out by betting 'without the favourite'. The Stewards' Cup on the first day was won by Lord Roseberry's Creole, on which I had a very welcome 2/- (10p) each way at 33/1, and the Goodwood Cup by multiple Royal Ascot winner Trelawny.

Then it was Epsom on the Saturday and Bank Holiday Monday, which unlike now was in early August. Here, the Moët & Chandon Silver Magnum, over the full Derby course and known as the Amateurs' Derby, was won by Thames Trader ridden by Mr John Lawrence, the renowned journalist who later became Lord Oaksey. With no convenient meeting to go to on the Tuesday, I had plenty of time to cycle to the next meeting, at Yarmouth, on the Wednesday. Meanwhile, I learned that I had been allocated an interview at Cambridge University. I didn't have much interest in going up to Cambridge, but the date they gave me was on the morning of a Newmarket race meeting, so as that meant I could stay in Queen's College the night before and then cycle off to Newmarket, just 13 miles away, afterwards, I thought that I should go to the interview. However, I was quite frank about the career I had chosen to pursue, so they decided that I was a non-trier and I wasn't offered a place, in spite of getting S^1 passes in Maths and Higher Maths and being beaten a short head in Physics with an S^2. So after another day at Newmarket, I arrived home two weeks after leaving Uppingham for the last time.

After a few days at home going to more local meetings, I was off on my travels again. Funds were severely limited, but most weeks I was able to go to four or five meetings a week (no Sundays then) for between £3 and £3/10/- (£3.50) a week – less than the price of a racecard now. Youth hostels were 3/6 (17½p) a night; transport was on bicycle; most hostels had self-catering facilities, so I carried food to cook in my pannier bags; racecards were 1/- (5p). Milk vending machines were then common sights outside a grocer's store and on a hot day, the chance to buy an ice-cold pint of milk for 6d (2½p) was very welcome. There were few motorways, and most main roads had a transport café every few miles, so if one looked unsuitable, there would be another one down the road. I sometimes used to judge a café by the price of tea, usually 4d or 6d, though a café in Newmarket called the Jockey's Café in Old Station Road charged only 3d (1.25p)! When I went to Leopardstown on a day trip to Ireland from Liverpool, without the bike, I saw that the price of tea in the Dublin bus station was 1/6 (7½p). 1/6! I said to myself, I'm not paying that much for a cuppa, so I went without!

The Youth Hostel Association of England & Wales ran well over 250 hostels throughout the country, generally concentrated in tourist areas rather than for proximity to racecourses. Buildings were mostly adapted from other uses, with a few purpose-built, and varied from huts to castles. Some were quite a distance from a public road and some lacked heating or even electricity and/or running water; sleeping accommodation was usually in bunk beds in dormitories, with blankets and pillows supplied, but it was necessary to bring or hire a towel and a cotton sleeping bag. They closed between 10am and 5pm, didn't allow arrival after 10pm and stays were limited to three consecutive nights. Most closed one night a week, which didn't always fit in with my needs for accommodation. They were intended mainly for ramblers, climbers and cyclists, and motorised tourists were barred; because I was always dressed for racing rather than cycle touring, I was often suspected of being ineligible to stay in them.

I jotted every item of expenditure in a notebook, which was a good discipline to control outgoings – even 2d to cycle over the Dunham toll bridge over the River Trent. Under 18s were not admitted free to racecourses then, so I had to go in the cheap rings or 'jimmy in' by climbing over a fence. Some courses were so easy to enter that way that I sometimes wondered whether that was so that people like me, who would otherwise not be able to go racing at all, could still come and buy a racecard. The main costs of cycling were replacement tyres (13/4) and inner tubes (6/8), so when I had to replace both, I had to find a whole £1 (gulp), a major blow to the budget! Most soft drinks were then sold in glass bottles with a returnable deposit, so whenever I spotted a discarded empty bottle, I could take it to any corner shop and reclaim the 3d, 4d, or if I was lucky, even 6d. Public telephones required the insertion of four pennies before dialling, with button A if the call was answered and button B to get a refund if there was no reply. Pressing button B sometimes hit the modest jackpot of 4d if the previous user had forgotten to reclaim his or her pennies.

The St Leger meeting at Doncaster was held on Tuesday to Friday at that time, with the St Leger on Wednesday. It was won at odds-on by Ragusa, trained by top Irish trainer Paddy Prendergast. After four days there I headed north, via a meeting at Sedgefield on the Saturday, to Scotland for the Scottish Circuit. This was a grouping of fixtures in the autumn that were arranged for the travelling circus that was racing in the days when road and rail journeys were much more time-consuming than now. Trainers from all over England would send horses to Scotland for the Autumn Circuit in September and the Summer Circuit in July, sometimes running twice or even three times before returning to their stables. Essex trainer Peter Poston always had plenty of runners, usually at 33-1, because he took full advantage of the travelling allowances then available, and was almost as interested in having runners as winners. The September meeting at Ayr, styled as the Royal Caledonian Hunt and Western Meeting, was a big social occasion for Scottish and Northern England racegoers, also attracting the biggest bookmakers of the day, not that I was in any position to partake in the society side, nor to trouble the main bookmakers

I attended Edinburgh, since renamed Musselburgh, on the Monday and Tuesday, and cycled the 80 miles over the Lowlands – which didn't seem very low at the time – for Ayr on the Wednesday, Thursday and Friday, and Bogside, just 10 miles away at Irvine but long since closed, on the Saturday. An unfortunate incident occurred at the

Ayr youth hostel when I stayed there. In the self-catering kitchen, hostellers kept their food in pigeon holes in the wall. I had some bacon that had gone missing and I looked for it to see if it had been moved to another pigeon hole. But someone had been pilfering other hostellers' food, and as I had been seen looking through the different food there, I fell under suspicion and my YHA card was retained. I had to join the Scottish Youth Hostels Association at Perth where I went racing on Wednesday and Thursday the following week, and my card was eventually returned only some time later. I found this very upsetting because I was accused of something that I not only didn't do but also wouldn't do. Ever since, I have been reluctant to assume anyone guilty just on circumstantial evidence.

Lanark racecourse had not yet closed, and Hamilton had no meeting that fortnight, so they would have to wait until I returned for the summer Scottish Circuit the following year. That winter I continued my tour of racecourses. On 7, 8 and 9 of November I went to the last ever meeting at Manchester, where there had been racing since 1687, including since 1902 at the Castle Irwell course – not actually in Manchester – named after the large house in whose original grounds it had been built. The main stand had been completed only the previous year, which accentuated the loss felt by the closure of the course, as did the poignancy of the racecard notice advertising the forthcoming sale of much of the course's equipment. The Manchester November Handicap, now run at Doncaster and still the last big race of the flat season proper, was won by Best Song, trained by Towser Gosden – father of present-day trainer John Gosden – who also trained runner-up Damredub, and throughout the meeting there was a close tussle between Lester Piggott and Scobie Breasley for the jockey's championship, narrowly decided in Scobie's favour.

Chapter 3

Gap year continues

Another rivalry was between Mill House, the previous season's impressive Cheltenham Gold Cup winner and said to be the best steeplechaser since multiple Gold Cup winner Golden Miller, and up-and-coming star Arkle, who had been equally impressive in the Broadway Chase at the same meeting. I was present when they met for the first time in the Hennessy Gold Cup, which Mill House won with Arkle in third place. But Arkle had slipped on landing over the third-last fence and many people still thought that Arkle would beat Mill House when they met in the Cheltenham Gold Cup. In any other era Mill House would have been recognised as one of the all-time greats, but was unfortunate to be a contemporary of the horse generally acknowledged as the greatest steeplechaser ever. But how lucky those of us in the early years of following racing were to witness the unfolding saga!

Cheltenham then was different from the present day. Jump racing was less popular than flat racing and attracted less betting and smaller crowds, but the National Hunt meeting, as the Festival was named, was still a big event and already drew large numbers from Ireland. There were but six races each day; two of them, the Foxhunters and National Hunt Chases, were run on a 4-mile course that started well behind the stands. Horses ran into a chute, roughly where the present horsewalk is, and jumped two fences before crossing the straight and joining the main course. The first circuit ran off the main course, round past the railway station and behind the stands; the runners would reappear at the top of the loop, which then ran past the winning post, through the present stables area and round the Best Mate enclosure for a final circuit round the New Course. Even the Gold Cup start took place out of view of the crowd in the stands, between the first two fences of the 4-mile course. Another peculiarity was that horses accessed the course via a pathway through the middle of the Tattersalls betting ring, with none of the segregation of horses and public of the present day! There were nearly as many hats as heads, with a significant proportion of bowlers, and the station was in full use, with special trains to and from London, Wolverhampton and Cardiff. I stayed at the youth hostel, which was in a hut way up Cleeve Hill and memorably cold.

The anticipation of the clash between Arkle and Mill House in the Gold Cup had been building since the previous March, only enhanced by the indecisive result at Newbury. The atmosphere when they eventually met again at Cheltenham was electric: many supporters of each horse wore the appropriate colours, which was rare at the time, and the cheers of encouragement started three-quarters of a mile out. Mill House started favourite of the four runners, which included previous Gold Cup winner Pas Seul; if there had been in-running betting[1] he would still have been favourite until before the second-last fence. Then the picture changed and Arkle came home in record time, a clear-cut winner of the first of his three Gold Cups to settle any doubts about his superiority.

The start of the Flat came soon after, with Monday, Tuesday and Wednesday at Lincoln, rapidly followed the same week by the three-day mixed meeting at Aintree, then known as Liverpool, with the Formula One Grand Prix motor racing circuit still in place alongside the turf course. I missed the Thursday at Aintree as it was an all-day journey over the Pennines, which are tough enough in any weather,

---

1. In-running betting is betting during a race. It was once common on course for a few bookmakers to call out odds during the running of a race, and now in-running betting is available on every race on betting exchanges.

Gap year continues

and I met every kind of bad weather there is in England: rain, hail, snow and, almost worst of all, headwinds. I was grateful that we don't have earthquakes or volcanoes in this country. Top weight for the Grand National was Pas Seul, well beaten by Arkle at Cheltenham, and the race was won by 12-year-old Team Spirit, giving trainer Fulke Walwyn and jockey Willie Robinson some compensation for the shock they had experienced with the defeat of Mill House; they also won the only other jump race on National day, the Liverpool Hurdle Handicap, with top weight Sempervivum.

After Cheltenham in April, several major midweek meetings followed in successive weeks: Newmarket Craven, Epsom Spring, Newmarket Spring and Chester. Newmarket featured the twenty-three-runner Free Handicap, now moribund, won by the Gordon Richards-trained Port Merion at the old-fashioned price of 100/8. Epsom, then a three-day meeting, included two handicaps dating from the mid-nineteenth century, The Great Metropolitan and City and Suburban, which are still run but no longer with the same prestige. The 'Great Met' was run over the defunct 2¼-mile course, which started near the winning post, ran the reverse way down the straight until crossing over the Downs to rejoin the main course before running down Tattenham Hill into the straight. At Newmarket the 2000 Guineas on Wednesday was won by French horse Baldric II, and the 1000 Guineas on Thursday by Irish horse Pourparler. After three days at Chester, followed by one at Haydock, I made a snap decision to make a day trip to Leopardstown, leaving the bike at Liverpool docks, and saw Ragusa, whom I had seen win the St Leger the previous year, win the main race.

After two weeks of lower-key meetings came York's Dante meeting, and the following week the four days of the Epsom Derby meeting. The first day on Tuesday featured another 2¼-mile race over the Downs, and the Derby was run on Wednesday, won by Irish horse Santa Claus ridden by Scobie Breasley. The Coronation Cup won by French horse Relko, under Yves Saint-Martin, was the main race on Thursday, followed on Friday by the Oaks, won by Homeward Bound with Greville Starkey up. On the Saturday before Royal Ascot I took the opportunity to see the Trooping of the Colour ceremony live on my way to Sandown, and the following Tuesday, cycling from Windsor youth hostel to Ascot, I caught sight of the then new stand from Swinley Bottom. Alas on the Thursday a cloudburst made the course waterlogged and the meeting was abandoned shortly before racing, leaving me to cycle to Warwick through further rain in time for the Friday evening meeting. Another trip to Ireland followed, this time taking the bike and staying at Dublin and Blessington youth hostels, to see Santa Claus follow up his Epsom win in the Irish Derby at The Curragh.

After the Eclipse Stakes at Sandown in early July, then open only to 3- and 4-year-olds and won by the aforementioned Ragusa from 2000 Guineas winner Baldric II, I returned to Scotland for the Scottish Summer Circuit in mid-July. Back in time for Goodwood, the rest of the summer was spent going to as many different courses as I could, and by September I had visited most British courses, including those that have since closed down: Alexandra Park, Birmingham, Bogside, Folkestone, Lanark, Lewes, Lincoln, Manchester, Stockton, Towcester and Wye. I carried on a bit beyond my eighteenth birthday as I wanted to go to Ludlow, after which it was time to go London to seek a job in the betting industry.

The bicycle I rode was a Raleigh touring model, with a 4-speed Sturmey-Archer gear mechanism, unlike the derailleur gears almost universal on more modern bikes. It had a dynamo to power the lights, and I fitted a speedometer so that I could monitor speed and distance travelled. My record distance in one hour was around 18½ miles and I once touched 48 mph down a long hill in Co. Durham. The record distance in a day was around 150 miles, which I refer to later, but distances of more than 100 miles in a day were common. In normal conditions I would reckon on averaging 12 mph, but I recall one ride from Skellingthorpe to York when I covered the 70 miles non-stop in five hours, an average of 14 mph. And I do mean non-stop, because the wheels never stopped turning; I thought I would have to stop when approaching the traffic lights in Bawtry, but they changed just in time and I was able to complete the journey without further threats to progress. Luckily I didn't need to cycle back home after racing. The longest I cycled on a raceday morning was the 85 miles from Skellingthorpe to Fakenham, then known as West Norfolk Hunt. When I did the Scottish Summer Circuit I left Lanark after racing on the Wednesday and arrived in Brighton, ready for Lewes and Goodwood, the following Sunday evening, stopping to sleep each of the four nights. Two clues there about how long ago that was!

My only foreign cycling trips, other than to The Curragh, were to Paris, once via Dover (taking in a meeting at Wye) and Calais, a two-day ride to Paris stopping overnight at Amiens youth hostel, and once via Newhaven and Dieppe, a one-day ride. I went racing at Longchamps, St Cloud, Maisons-Laffitte, Auteuil and Vincennes (trotting). Cycling around a city amongst cars where only the passengers have steering wheels takes a bit of getting used to, but the only mishap was en route to Longchamps when I was knocked off my bike by the chauffeur-driven Israeli ambassador to France; I was unhurt, but my attempted insurance claim for a torn jacket came to naught.

Cycling long distances is usually physically demanding, but mentally relaxing. There was far less motor traffic then, and the main enemy was bad weather – and punctures. Mending a puncture is easy, but what is difficult is locating the hole and they are particularly unwelcome when it is dark or wet – or both. Another time I cycled from Lichfield to Shrewsbury on a very hot sunny day with my shirt off; I didn't realise how sunburnt my back had been until I got into bed that night; I was sore for days. I recall cycling through thick freezing fog one dark night trying to find Ilam Hall hostel for Uttoxeter. When I finally arrived, I was shocked to find that my hair felt like a steel hawser because of the frozen fog in it. I am sometimes asked how in later years I coped with the inevitable losing runs and, reflecting on my cycling days, I think the necessary resilience may have been formed then. When I was several miles from home or my next hostel, dark and cold, and my legs were turning to jelly, there was no choice but to carry on. Such experience is often described as character-forming, which is a euphemism for very tough going.

Looking back, I can't think of a better way to have spent a gap year. In spite of the punctures and other problems with the bike, and the rain and the cold, it's mostly the better memories that linger: the variety of countryside and townscapes and people; Midland towns bedecked with trolley bus wires; dingy betting shops, light years away from present-day shops, where no one questioned my age; milk vending machines dispensing 6d pints of ice-cold milk; transport cafés in abundance. During my Tour of Britain, my determination to be a bookmaker had been refined into wanting to be a racecourse bookmaker; I had little idea what path I would have to take to achieve that end, but I knew I would have to start at the bottom.

Chapter 4

First job and first coursing meeting

My father had somehow found me a place to live in London's South Kensington in a hall of residence for junior civil servants. Once I had settled in there, I set about searching for my first venture into the regular world of bookmaking. I touted myself round several bookmakers in Central London, when they were far more plentiful than before they were gradually swallowed up by the public companies. But when I proudly showed prospective employers my exam certificates, most thought I was over-qualified, and probably suspected that I did not intend to stay with them for long. Eventually I applied to the firm of Hunter Simmonds, which owned a group of bookmaking firms trading under different names: as well as Hunter Simmonds, there was Beresford & Smith, based in the West End, Heathorns, based in the City of London, Joe Lee, David Rae, and others.

I was interviewed in the West End office by the manager, Frank Young, a hard-bitten Yorkshireman. I think he was rather impressed when he asked me, out of the blue in the middle of the conversation, what a sixteenth of £1 was and I immediately answered one and threepence. The interview continued and at the end of it he offered me a job at £15 a week, which I readily accepted. After a few weeks in their betting shop in nearby Maddox Street, which ceased to be a betting shop many years ago, I was brought back into their credit office on the top floor of a building near the Piccadilly end of Old Bond Street (fortunately there was a lift!). In those days, betting information and results came into the office one letter at a time via a ticker-tape machine of the type now seen only in old films set in stockbrokers' offices.

I soon realised that Beresford & Smith was one of the larger credit offices in London. The firm was owned by three sons of the eponymous Hunter Simmonds – Charles, who rarely appeared in the office, Ernest, who was in charge and there most days, and Sid, who was usually bumbling around the office doing not very much. They also had offices in other towns, in particular Bournemouth, managed by Ernest's son Michael. They also had racecourse rails pitches at most racecourses in the south of England, being represented mainly by Jack Hawkins, Arthur Holloway and John Smith.

My job was to answer telephones and write down the bets punters were ringing for, and to settle (i.e. calculate winnings) bets, which involved learning all the short cuts for calculating various prices, such as a third plus a third for 4/9, or a half plus one-fifteenth for 8/15. There was also the block method for working out multiple bets, which removed the need to calculate them separately and then add up all the individual doubles, etc. in such bets as yankees. I made no secret of the fact that I wanted to work on the racecourse for the firm, but apart from occasionally being high up in the grandstand at Ascot with manager Nobby Rodford, did so only once when John Smith and I caught the train to Wincanton one rainy November day, changing at Templecombe for the now long-closed Wincanton station. Ernie Simmonds seemed to have a soft spot for me, so it was a serious blow to my prospects when we all arrived at the office to learn that he had been killed in a car crash the previous evening. Soon his son Michael took over running the office, but he didn't have a soft spot for me or anyone else – nor me for him. The office moved premises to a newer building in Newman Street, off Oxford Street, but I didn't enjoy working there as much as I had at Old Bond Street.

I realised that I didn't look likely to get on the racecourse with them, so it was time to leave after eighteen months there and resume my racecourse tours. On my last day we were sending out the weekly

First job and first coursing meeting

accounts, all hand written and addressed, and as I wanted to get a particular train home to Lincoln, I was working flat out to get that job finished. I well remember office manager Frank Young remarking that it looked as if I was applying for a raise, rather than leaving. He also warned me that I was unlikely to achieve my ambition of becoming a bookmaker, not because he hoped I wouldn't but because he thought I didn't have the necessary toughness to do so. He underestimated my determination and it is one of my greatest regrets that he died of cancer before I was able to prove him wrong.

I would usually cycle the 18 miles from Brookmans Park near Hatfield, where I was living with my Aunt Nora, to the office, taking ninety minutes. Thanks to the speedometer, I got to know the distances between all the major junctions on the route into London, and would know exactly what time I should be at each point to reach the office by 10 am. There were days when I didn't feel up to the ride, especially if the rain was pouring down. I also often used to cycle to the races on my days off, sometimes going straight from the office the evening before to a youth hostel on the way to the course.

The longest distance I ever covered in a day was when Arkle won his third Gold Cup at 1/10. Having cycled straight from the office to Oxford youth hostel the evening before, I cycled the 50 miles to Cheltenham before racing, and after racing the 100 miles back to Brookmans Park. A memorable day out, but I knew I'd been for a bike ride by the time I got home in the small hours of the next morning. One of the most frightening experiences I remember was cycling towards Crockham Hill hostel for Lingfield one dark rainy night down a long winding hill when the brakes were too wet to function and the front light gave little visibility of the road ahead. Somehow I managed to reach the bottom of the hill without mishap, apart from being soaked.

It was towards the end of my time at Beresford & Smith that I discovered coursing. I used to read about it in the Sporting Life, and the Waterloo Cup results would come in on the ticker tape. It was difficult to make head or tail of how the sport worked just from written reports and results, so I resolved to go and see for myself. The first opportunity to do so came at a meeting of the North Herts. Coursing Club at Litlington, near Royston. I cycled from Brookmans Park early in the morning of a day off to what most coursing followers would describe as the worst meeting to attend as an introduction to coursing. But I loved it! I had been greyhound racing before, first at Hendon track, now occupied by Brent Cross Shopping Centre, and later at White City and elsewhere, but coursing was by contrast such a natural sport in open countryside and a much better all-round test of a greyhound. It was a walked-up meeting where the crowd and dogs walk up and down the available fields until they find a hare, as opposed to the more usual driven meetings where a team of beaters walk up adjoining fields and drive hares into the field where coursing takes place. I walked all day over ploughed fields and though not many hares were found (as was usual at North Herts.), I thoroughly enjoyed my day out watching a natural sport in natural countryside, and to top it up field manager Ron Hemmings gave me £2 for acting as a beater, and I and my bike got a lift most of the way home in the back of a dog van. My next meeting was completely different. I hitch-hiked up the A1 to the first day of the Huntingdon Silver Stakes, being picked up in a Landrover for the last few miles by Jane Clayton, sister of Newmarket racehorse trainer Jack Clayton. This was a driven meeting, one of the biggest in the coursing calendar. It was held in the 100-acre field at Buckworth near Huntingdon, attended by a large crowd, including bookmakers.

Chapter 5

Back on the road, first racecourse job, every course on a bike and photofinish betting

Back in the big wide world, I lost no time in resuming going racing, as having left Beresford & Smith on Maundy Thursday and moved back to Skellingthorpe, I was at Doncaster on Easter Saturday (no Good Friday racing back then). With no income in prospect I still had to be very careful what I spent, but at least I had some money saved up, which was just as well, as the overnight charge at youth hostels had risen to 4/- (20p)! I had also been saving my luncheon vouchers. These were worth a few shillings each, which employers could give to their staff tax free to be used at the many catering outlets of various types that accepted them. I had a booklet that listed all the cafés and restaurants throughout the country where they were accepted.

At this point I still hadn't managed to get to all the British racecourses, and although the priority was to break into working in the course side of the bookmaking profession, Bangor, with no grandstand and only five fixtures, and Cartmel, then with only two days racing a year at the Whitsun Bank Holiday, had been elusive. They were duly ticked off in May; I had already been to Chepstow, via the old ferry from Aust to Beachley before the Severn Bridge was built, but it wasn't until several years later that I got round to cycling there to complete the cycling tour of all the country's courses at that time.

From Bicycle to Bentley, A Bookmaker's Story

Early in the twentieth century there had been talk about new racecourses in various locations, such as Fairlop and Llantrisant, which would mean I would have to cycle to them to keep up the record, but they all came to naught. Then Great Leighs, since renamed Chelmsford, opened. I had already cycled up the A12 aged 16 on my way to Yarmouth, but I had failed to foresee that the Essex Showground would eventually become a racecourse, so to maintain the record, at the dyslexic age of 61 I had only to take the bike on the train to Chelmsford and cycle the eight miles to Great Leighs and back. Ffos Las was a bigger challenge. I had already cycled as far as Severn Tunnel Junction station, so I was able to maintain continuity by travelling by train there and cycling the 90-odd miles to Ffos Las, stopping at Bridgend overnight. I then thought that I should cycle to the two Northern Irish courses, Down Royal and Downpatrick, to complete the UK set, so I chose the only time of year when they had fixtures a few days apart and, taking in a meeting at Ayr on the way to Stranraer, sailed with the bike to Belfast. This meant that I hadn't covered the entire journey by bike, but my excuse is that I couldn't find a snorkel long enough.

I considered that I had done well to cycle to Ffos Las at the age of 63 until I read about an Irish man who cycled from his home in Clonmel on a pilgrimage to the holy site of Knock at the age of 90. It took him four days to cover the 130 miles, but I was so impressed that I have kept the cutting about him in the hope that it will inspire me when I reach that age. Meanwhile, I am hoping that the next racecourse to open is at somewhere like KeyNshaM[1], just a few miles from home.

One ride I remember from 1966 was going home from the Chester May meeting to Skellingthorpe after the end of the third day.

---

1. Radio Luxembourg listeners will recall Horace Bachelor, who advertised his Infra-draw system in pre-lottery days, when backing draws on football pools fuelled dreams of sudden wealth. When reading out his address for punters to subscribe, he always emphasised the 'n' and 'm' in Keynsham.

Back on the road, first racecourse job

The infamous Moors Murders trial had been taking place at Chester Assizes near the racecourse all week, and the route took me past Saddleworth Moor, where the young victims of Ian Brady and Myra Hindley had been buried. By the time I got there, it was twilight, and I could see where the police had been digging looking for bodies – really spooky.

After Cartmel on the Bank Holiday Monday, it was on to Redcar on Tuesday, followed by Newcastle Wednesday evening, after which I bit off more than I could chew. I could not get to a youth hostel before closing time, so I decided I would cycle through the night to Carlisle for racing on Thursday evening, stay at Carlisle hostel that night and on to Ayr for Friday evening. I made it to Carlisle in time, but come Friday, I was so tired that it was a struggle to get to Ayr, and I arrived too exhausted and too late for the races, and had to be content with Ayr's meeting on Saturday.

Later that summer I met up with Noel Wray, a bookmaker based in Harrogate who had rails pitches at several northern courses, and clerked for him for a few months. With many fewer fixtures than nowadays, the work was fairly sporadic, but it was great to get started again in my chosen profession – or should that be vocation? I still didn't know how I was going to progress to independence with limited capital; would I find someone to finance me? Could I gradually make my way into the ring and progress gradually? At that stage I wasn't aiming to become a leading bookmaker, I just wanted to be a surviving bookmaker.

I was now free to go to plenty of coursing meetings in that winter's coursing season. Because of both the weather and the early starts – usually 9 or 9.30 am – cycling was impractical and I usually hitchhiked around the country. I was sometimes suspected of being an 'anti', attending only to gather propaganda against coursing, but gradually became accepted for the enthusiast that I was, and finally got to my first Waterloo Cup, the Derby of coursing, in 1967. Cheltenham and Aintree followed, where I saw Red Rum dead-heat in a five-furlong selling plate, and Foinavon take advantage of being the worst horse in the Grand National to win at 100-1 after the pile-up at the twenty-third fence.

Not long after that I had been introduced to Dickie Gaskell, Ladbrokes' principal racecourse representative, by George Vickers, a professional punter who lived in the Swallowbeck part of our parish, and I started with that firm at Nottingham in April. The main part of my job was to enable communication between office and course. The only way to do this in the days before mobile phones changed the world was via a public phone kiosk, so my instructions were to join the queue for the box, get in five minutes before each race, ring the office and keep the line open until the off to relay any messages to and from the office; and then stay in the queue for the next race. The flaw in this arrangement was that many courses had only a few phone boxes, or even only one, and there were several other firms trying to do the same thing, and it was necessary to co-operate with each other to avoid being physically yanked out of the phone box.

George Vickers would describe my position as 'the lowest form of life at Ladbrokes', which was a fairly accurate job description, but it was a start, and I hoped to progress. Meanwhile, I had bought my first car, a Morris 1100, and was learning to drive. I got a lot of driving practice with George as accompanying driver on journeys to racecourses, often with other passengers, including Tommy Weston who rode two Derby winners – Hyperion and Sansovino for Lord Derby – and Tim Molony, multiple champion jump jockey. I eventually passed my driving test at the fourth attempt, and after a summer travelling all over the country, including Scotland, for Ladbrokes by train or car, moved back to London to share a flat with a few friends.

I had hoped by now to have been given a chance as a clerk, and when I went to see Gerald Green, Cyril Stein's cousin who was in charge of Ladbrokes' head office in Ganton Street, he said I would do so in time, but this didn't materialise, as they kept getting young guys from the office who weren't particularly good at it. So I remained on the lowest rung until one day at Chepstow the following March.

There was a solitary phone box at Chepstow, with three or four people trying to use it in the same way, as well as the general public. One particular race, I was duly on the phone five minutes before the off, which was something of a feat in itself, but had to relinquish it before the off to avoid an ignominious and possibly violent exit from the box. After the race it transpired that the course team had missed a message, and when the rep Peter George rang the office he came back with the message that I had got the sack. On the drive back along the M4 home to Chiswick, it gradually dawned on me that, far from being a disaster, I now had the opportunity to progress elsewhere, which I clearly wasn't going to do with Ladbrokes. I recall that when I told one of my flatmates what had happened, he said I wasn't sounding like someone who had just lost his job. When I asked Peter George some years later why I had been sacked, his reply was 'Mind your own business', which seemed a strange comment on a matter that was very much my business.

I carried on going racing regularly, as I knew it was important to be seen regularly if I was to have any chance of picking up any jobs on the course. I was already used to minimising expenses, but I needed to win enough by betting to stay afloat. Around this time I realised that there was money to be made by betting on photo-finishes. By standing on the finish line and concentrating on the finish of each race, it was often possible to back the winner, especially if a well-backed horse was second, as bookmakers liked to hedge and were happy to let me bet £100 to win £2 or £3 even if it wasn't close. There were a few other regular unofficial judges, but we all managed to make it pay, though we had to be wary. A bet was on the result of the race, not just the result of the photo-finish, and there were a lot more disqualifications for interference, etc. than nowadays. There was also another way to lose, which fortunately I was not a victim of. One day at Brighton, a horse had clearly won by about a neck, and the usual judges confidently backed it at 20/1 on. It prevailed in the photo, but there had been a false start; this meant a rerun of the race in which it didn't run, but under the rules at the time, any horse that had come under starter's orders was a runner, so the bets were lost.

I think betting on photos really sharpened me up, which is a necessary attribute for working in the betting ring. Unlike the present day when the announcement of the winner comes much sooner and would be 'Here is the result of the second race. Winner number 1', it would be a sudden death announcement, 'Winner number 1', possibly preceded by the click of the loudspeaker system if we were lucky, so we never knew how much time we had to get any bets on. Also, when the winning line was in Members and some distance from the betting ring, racing officials didn't like to see punters moving without the due decorum they thought appropriate, so I just had to imitate contestants in a walking race. It was amazing how many friends I suddenly had when there was a close finish in a big race and they all wanted to know what I thought had won!

Sometimes if the horses were wide apart at somewhere like Newmarket, it was possible to get on a horse that had won by anything up to a length, but at Newton Abbot one day I got on when the winning distance was ten lengths! Two horses were fighting out the finish, but the jockey was gradually falling off one of them, and no one knew whether he had come off before the line or after it. But I knew that the other horse had got there first anyway, so I backed it accordingly, and the camera revealed that the other jockey had come off too soon and was therefore not a finisher, with ten lengths back to the second-placed horse. Another time at Ascot a horse was announced as the winner without a photo, and as I ambled back to the ring, Victor Chandler (senior), in the no. 1 pitch in Tattersalls, was calling it at evens. The angle from there was so deceptive that everyone thought a mistake had been made, but I rapidly had an even £25 with Victor, and I think he was grateful that I had put him right and stopped him laying a much bigger bet to someone else.

Back on the road, first racecourse job

Before getting going on photo betting I had been pottering around winning a bit here and losing a bit there, and after a few months I was beginning to wonder whether I could keep going like that. Then in May there was a horse running called Gold Pollen, which belonged to Bill Gaskin, a prominent coursing man, and I somehow picked up the vibes that it was well fancied. I had £25 to £4 and £5 each way at 11/2 and it duly won. The figures might seem rather puny now, but at the time it meant a lot, and gave me the encouragement (and the readies) to carry on.

At Royal Ascot, Song won the New Stakes on the third day. Luckily for me, rain had cleared most of the Royal Enclosure crowd from in front of the stand, so not only did I have a clear view of the finish but it was also much easier than usual to get out to the ring. I had £75 to win £25 and £100 to win £20, which was most of the tank at the time, but I had no worries about collecting. It wasn't all plain sailing though. In the Eclipse the next month, I was sure that Taj Dewan had beaten Royal Palace and bet £100 to win £20 and £30 to win £10; I was wrong. The Sporting Life the next day reported that 'hardened punters scrambled to bet the odds on Taj Dewan', and later that year one journalist wrote that hearing Royal Palace announced the winner was one of the best moments of the year for him. I didn't consider myself a hardened punter, but I had scrambled to bet odds on the loser, and that announcement was one of my worst moments of the year. I went home feeling not very happy, but over the weekend I realised that things could be a lot worse; I didn't owe anyone, and I still had my health, so I picked myself up and carried on, going to the Newmarket July meeting the following week.

Chapter 6

Apprenticeship, on the dole, first licence and pitches

As 1968 wore on, the policy of going to the races as often as possible to be seen started to pay off. Still based in London, I was going mostly to southern meetings, with the occasional forays to the north. I would still cycle to the nearer meetings, but otherwise travel either by car or train. I was now driving an Austin Cambridge, a more solid car than my first car, with a proper chassis, but disaster struck when the engine developed a serious problem with a broken piston. The estimate for its repair was more than I could afford, so the only option was to repair it myself. I had no garage, so it had to be done parked in the road in Chiswick; I bought the Haynes manual for the model and set about it myself. It was a cold winter to be in the street underneath the car, but over several weeks interspersed with days at the races I was able to dismantle the engine, buy the necessary parts, reassemble it all and resume driving it.

The expenses of going racing were funded mainly by photo-finish betting. No full-time racecourse position presented itself, but I was able to secure the occasional day's work, and eventually I was taken on by various bookmakers who didn't have enough pitches to offer more than part-time work. The standard daily wage was £5 and expenses, with occasional honours of a few pounds when results had been good.

I went up to Ayr for the Western meeting in September, where the Ladbrokes representative, George Taiano, signed me on for the

Apprenticeship, on the dole, first licence and pitches

three days. My function was the same as in my previous employment as 'the lowest form of life', enabling communication between office and course pitch. The first day went smoothly, but in the evening when George spoke to the office, he was told that he mustn't employ me, so he reluctantly had to give me the sack from Ladbrokes for the second time.

Having paid for National Insurance stamps when I was working in London, I wanted to take full advantage of them and so I signed up for the dole. Dole was quite easy to qualify for; you could specify what sort of job you wanted, and where you wanted it, and you then had to sign on in the labour exchange once a week to prove that you were available for work – so you could say you wanted to work as a lighthouse keeper and you wanted to work in central Birmingham. I really was looking for work and said I wanted a job as a racecourse bookmaker's clerk anywhere in the country, but the chance of being found such a position by the labour exchange was extremely remote. I felt somewhat embarrassed when I went to Windsor one day and popped into the silver ring where, wearing my junior members' badge, I bumped into one of the staff from the dole office on his day off.

On days when I didn't have any pre-arranged jobs, I would go racing in 'gizza-job' mode and hawk myself round the ring hoping to get work for that day. There were many more course bookmakers then, and the chance of finding work in this way was reasonably high. Sometimes it would be just for the day, but as I became known as a competent clerk or floorman, jobs became more frequent. The function of a floorman was to keep the bookmaker up to date with everyone else's odds, keeping him informed immediately of any sudden rush for a price elsewhere, and placing any hedging bets required. Happily, most of the bookmakers I worked for were tolerant of my photo-finish betting sideline, so I was usually able to drop the book on the off and make the mad dash to the finishing line.

Clerking involved writing all the bets in a specially ruled ledger with a column for each runner (the book), keeping a running total of the total potential payout on each horse and of the total money taken on the race (the field money), so that the bookmaker could see at a glance which horses he needed to lay more and which horses he needed to steer clear of laying. This required neatness and accuracy at speed, and the ability to do mental arithmetic quickly, all the while concentrating on what the bookmaker was calling amid the general hubbub of the racecourse, possibly in driving rain with the public brushing by. At busy times it would be necessary to concentrate on recording the bets and complete the running totals when it quietened down, or even estimate them and add them precisely after the race to arrive at an exact profit or loss on the race and on the day.[1] Some bookmakers were better at calling the bets than others; when later I became the one calling the bets, I prided myself on calling bets clearly and in the proper format. For instance, if a punter was having £35 at 11/4, I would call 96¼ to 35, whereas some would call £35 at 11/4, leaving the clerk to calculate it. Modern clerks need a different set of skills, the main new one being total familiarity with the computer system, of which there are several, being used.

At that time the tic-tac sign language was widely used to relay prices and bets from one enclosure to another, or within rings, and at larger meetings, there were up to half a dozen self-employed 'public' tic-tac men positioned by the rails handling trading between the rails, which was the wholesale end of the betting market, and ring bookmakers, many of whom employed a man just to read the prices and trade through the public tic-tacs. I taught myself tic-tac by watching other workers using it, but as with any language there is quite a gulf between learning the vocabulary and becoming fluent. I rarely worked as a tic-tac, but one day at Cheltenham I did

---

1. See betting appendix for explanation of how bets and liabilities were written in the ledger.

Apprenticeship, on the dole, first licence and pitches

so for Eddie Baxter from Glastonbury, who traded as Avalon Turf Investments. During the betting on one race, I mis-read 11/4 as 100/30, which encouraged him to lay the horse in question at 3/1, thinking he was earning by hedging at 100/30. Fortunately, the horse lost, and he never knew about my bungle.

One of the bookmakers I sometimes worked for was Vic Gardner, who had a betting shop in Marlborough and a few course pitches. He had been a jockey riding winners for George Todd, to whom he had been apprenticed, and others, including in India. His father, Ted Gardner, had been one of the top jockeys of his day, riding for Lord Derby. It is thought that there had been only three triple dead-heats before the advent of the photo-finish camera, and Ted Gardner had been involved in two of them. On the way back from Chepstow late in 1970, we stopped off at Bristol dogs, on the site of what is now an Ikea store at Eastville, and then shared with Bristol Rovers Football Club. One of the bookmakers in the second ring, known as the tote end, was about to give up his pitch and we decided we would go into equal partnership and apply for the pitch. I had managed to amass a small amount of capital by then, by dint of hard saving and a few successful share trades, and we started in November of that year. Unlike present times, greyhound tracks were restricted to two meetings per week and eight races per meeting, with extra meetings allowed on bank holidays, so it didn't restrict me from going horse racing too much.

So now I was a bookmaker, albeit not in my own name, but still an important point in my career. The next step would be to apply for my own licence, which I did early the following year at the age of 24, an unusually young age for someone with no family connection to the profession. Compared to all the rigmarole and red tape facing present-day applicants, this was quite an easy process. I was required to place an advertisement, stating that I was applying to the local magistrates for a bookmakers' permit, in any newspaper circulating in my local area in case anyone wanted to object – I chose the Sporting

Life, as most applicants did – and to notify the police and Customs & Excise. I then had to appear before the magistrates at a meeting of their betting licensing committee, and answer a few simple questions about experience and financial soundness, so that they could decide whether I was a 'fit and proper person' to be granted a permit.

They agreed that I was, so I obtained my permit on 2 February 1971, just in time to bet for the first time in my own name at that year's Waterloo Cup[2] at Altcar near Southport. It was always notoriously wet or cold, or usually both, at Altcar, with frequent delays for hours or even days for frost. Once a member of the crowd felt so sorry for me standing in pouring rain that he brought me a glass of hot Ribena, which was very welcome. The ultimate symptom of global warming was not the melting of polar ice-caps but when in later years an ice cream van would come to trade at Waterloo Cups. I didn't make a profit at my first attempt, but it was a start.

The next step was to apply for pitches on the racecourse. Waiting lists for Tattersalls pitches were long, so I had to start with a few minor ring pitches, mostly local but also at Chester and York, and point-to-points, at the end of the line. I also went to make a book at the lesser coursing meetings, where you could usually count the number of bookmakers on the thumbs of one hand (i.e. just me). Meanwhile, I continued to work for other bookmakers so that I was not reliant on my own bookmaking to subsist. This was necessary as the end of the line in minor rings is a very hard place to attempt to make a profit. We used to clerk in shillings, so if someone had £1 at 7/2 I would call the bet to the clerk not as 3½ to 1 but as 70 to 20, which gives a clue as to how meagre turnover could be. When Eric won the Chester Cup in 1972, I laid it only once – £1 at 33/1 – but that was enough to make it a losing race.

Waiting lists were very slow-moving, partly because bookmakers seemed to take a long time to die, but mainly because of the iniquitous

---

2. See Coursing Appendix for more about coursing and the Waterloo Cup.

practice of 'sticking-in'. Some bookmakers who lacked either the nerve or the finance to bet with their own money would find someone to provide the necessary funds to operate, thus jumping the waiting list. Some were even rumoured to have five shareholders of 25% each, rather like the impresarios in the film The Producers. I found this very frustrating, especially as pitch committees, consisting of members of local bookmakers' associations who were tasked with the job of administering pitches, lacked the will to tackle the problem, which was not solved until the buying and selling of picks was allowed.

The position of a bookmaker's pitch was, and is, crucial to its viability. One of the provisions of the pitch rules book was that a bookmaker new to a ring had to attend 75% of the fixtures at that course before he could gain a seniority date and qualify for a permanent pitch, whereby he could move up as others dropped out, or take advantage of any temporary move-ups if other bookmakers were absent. One day in the cheap ring in the middle of Stratford, the pitches for the day were being allocated before racing when one bookmaker was asked whether he had qualified for a permanent pitch. I vented my frustration by remarking that he had been unable to keep a sticker-in for long enough to qualify, at which he expressed his anger by knocking me over! He later apologised and we shook hands.

Travelling the 120 miles from home in London to Bristol, while the M4 was still under construction, twice a week was too much, even though I would often stay in Marlborough to break the journey up. With the help of an estate agent that Vic knew in the Wiltshire town of Devizes, I found a one-bedroom flat on the edge of that town in 1971. It was a newly built housing association property, which meant that the rent I was paying went some way towards owning a share of it, so that when I left it, I would receive some funds as part-owner, which was very useful when I later came to buy a house in Bath. It was still about 35 miles from Eastville, but reduced travelling miles and time considerably. After a couple of years or so, Vic decided he would rather concentrate on his betting shop, so I took over the pitch and bet in my own name there.

I carried on mixing working on my own few pitches with working for other bookmakers for a few years, after which I had got into Tattersalls, first at Chepstow and Ascot in 1972, and then at Yarmouth in 1973. I soon discovered why the Yarmouth pitch had materialised so soon – apart from being so far away, making staffing difficult, the market there was very volatile, making it nearly impossible in the back line not to get caught out with prices. With a handful of poor pitches and Eastville and coursing meetings not providing much in the way of profits, I needed to carry on with photo-finish betting, but when my local Inland Revenue man wanted to know how I was surviving, I had great difficulty explaining how it worked, and convincing him that I could make a profit from such betting. I eventually persuaded him that I didn't actually lose at it, and he insisted I keep detailed records of photo bets, even though as betting winnings they were not taxable.

At Ascot I decided to try betting without the favourite. This was betting on which horse either wins or finishes second to the favourite, a variation very popular in Ireland. It was described in the pitch rules book as unorthodox betting and offered on most days at midland and northern courses, but rarely seen on southern courses. I compiled a chart to tell me what price horses should be, taking into account its odds in the full market and the odds of the favourite that I was betting without, But before I had much chance either to test the viability of that approach or get more Tattersalls pitches in the south to establish betting 'best of the rest' in the south, I was approached with a job offer that, although I didn't realise it at the time, was to change the direction of my career.

Chapter 7

In at the deep end and early policy decisions

Thomas Henry Dey was an office and racecourse bookmaker who operated at southern courses in the 1920s and 1930s. T.H. Dey was probably the first bookmaker to be the subject of a book, Leaves From A Bookmaker's Book, which he wrote himself around 1931 and is an amusing tale of his career with many anecdotes. His photo reveals that he did not seem to be a stereotypical bookmaker, but looked rather bookish, and the volume is peppered with quotations from Shakespeare. One which seems to have inspired him was from Julius Caesar: 'There is a tide in the affairs of men, which, taken at the flood, leads on to fortune'. This could be translated into modern parlance as 'when you're in form, crack on', but he omits to mention that Brutus, whose line it is, commits suicide later in the play! Dey started as a junior shorthand writer in the bookmaking office of notorious gambler Bob Sievier, owner of quadruple classic winner Sceptre, who, when it was put to him during a court case that he was a gambler pure and simple, responded that he might be pure, but he was not simple.

Not many racegoers in the 1970s would have heard of him, but his name lived on in a firm that had a few rails pitches at the major courses in the south. One day in the summer of 1972 its proprietor, Keith Higgs, collared me at a race meeting and asked me if I would like to represent the firm on the rails, and I accepted the offer. Keith was a cousin of my former boss Michael Simmonds, though it seemed that they were not the best of friends. Pitch rules then current stipulated that no pitch holder could represent another bookmaker, so to avoid my having to surrender the few pitches I had, the arrangement was that Keith would be the pitch holder, trading as Thomas Henry Dey, and his nephew Michael Higgs would be the nominated representative. Our first meeting on the rails was Ascot on 6 April 1973, and I was to be paid £10 a day after travel and entrance expenses, plus a share of profits – if there were any. Sometimes Keith would come to the races and stand on the pitch himself with me clerking, but more usually I would be there with Michael as clerk, catering to some regular clients, without trying to make a big splash in the market. Accounts were dealt with by the office, and I would find a telephone box on the way home to ring the individual bets through.

The latter-day incarnation of the Dey firm was operating in the time when rails bookmakers were not allowed to display their prices. We had either to call out our odds or wait for someone to come and ask the odds for their fancy. Having some regular clients and account holders was thus far more necessary than it was for the cash bookmakers in the ring. Indeed, some rails bookmakers would not even accept cash bets, betting exclusively to their own credit clients.

After betting at Ascot, Newbury and Sandown throughout the summer, the Southern Association, which administered pitches at those courses, decided that I was acting as the representative, even though Michael was the approved rep. They therefore intended to apply the relevant rule to remove me from those pitches I had in my own name. One solution discussed was for me to apply to replace Keith as pitch holder for those pitches, together with Salisbury, Goodwood, Cheltenham, Chepstow and Wincanton, but after much correspondence with the Southern Association, we abandoned that idea and carried on as before, and I accepted the forfeiture of my own few pitches – no great loss.

In April 1974, Keith decided that he wanted to bet only at Ascot, Newbury and Sandown, and asked me whether I wanted to continue in those circumstances, so I had to contemplate my next step. The rule that no bookmaker with a pitch could represent another bookmaker was clear, and I had no intention of challenging it, but some pitch committees interpreted the rule to mean that I also had to quit my waiting list positions. I challenged this successfully and remained on the Tattersalls lists for the several courses I had applied for, although I was still a very long way from the top of any list.

It would clearly take many years to work my way up waiting lists for Tattersalls pitches, and even more years to move up in the ring to half-viable pitches. I couldn't take over the Dey pitches, but waiting lists for rails pitches were either non-existent or very short, and the churn of rails bookmakers was even more pronounced than the stagnation in the ring. So I could apply for rails pitches, and at least I would be starting with some of the Dey clients I had been dealing with. I knew I would be jumping in at the deep end, and that I would either learn to swim or drown. Most other bookmakers thought I was doomed, and neither I nor anyone else imagined that within a decade or so I would be taking six-figure bets (nine figures if you count the .00!). As well as the courses where I had bet for T.H. Dey, I applied for rails pitches at other western, southern and midland courses that had rails; even Cheltenham required only a short wait. My first venture in the deep end on the rails was at Chepstow on 29 June 1974, quickly followed the next Saturday by Bath; at this stage I was treading water, concentrating on survival.

The apprenticeship I had served had been an excellent grounding. I don't know how many different bookmakers I worked for in those half-dozen years, but seeing so many different approaches to the business was great experience. I observed that those who had opinions, whether based on form study or supposed information, didn't seem to do as well as those who relied on the figures (i.e. the inbuilt percentages) to make it pay, so I resolved to take the mathematical approach. I reasoned that you could spend all night studying a race and conclude that the second favourite would beat the favourite, but if something came to beat them both, you would have missed out, even if you were right. I would rather try to make a small percentage of a large turnover, though it would be some time before I could claim a large turnover.

Two other principles that I adopted early on were not to worry if turnover was not forthcoming, but to be patient and wait to lay horses at the right price, and to accept any size bet asked for, within reason, even if it meant having to hedge at a lower price. I recall one day at Wincanton when I didn't take any bets until the fourth race; but over the next few years several other bookmakers, including the national firms, came and went on the rails there and I outlasted them. And I never took any heed of the multitude of racing superstitions, such as lucky mascots or clothes, seeing magpies on the way to the races, see hay you'll pay, see straw you'll draw, driving under a railway bridge as a train passes (is it lucky if you're on a train as a car goes under a bridge?), green being unlucky (stick to all-weather courses), back the first trainer you see at the course, etc, etc. How does any horse know what you're wearing or have seen on the way? The only superstition I believe in is about seeing a funeral on the way to the races, which is definitely unlucky for whoever is in the coffin.

The exception to not studying form was when I went coursing, where I couldn't follow the market as I did at the races, as I *was* the market, usually being the only bookmaker there. But studying the results published in instalments throughout the season by the National Coursing Club, and making my own notes on the coursing I saw at most of the main meetings, enabled me to price up courses reasonably sensibly. Sometimes I reported on meetings myself when the usual reporter was absent – there can't be many betting sports where the bookie helps to write the form book!

Some coursing meetings involved trudging from one field to another during the day. One of the many Irish priests who used to frequent coursing meetings once remarked that seeing me carrying the joint (the old-fashioned bookmaker's tripod stand, satchel and board) over a ploughed field reminded him of Christ carrying his cross; I often felt that it was indeed a heavy burden I had to bear, especially when I was getting soaked with very little prospect of any profit.

It was through coursing that I got to know John McCririck. In 1972 Harry Arnold, coursing correspondent of the Sporting Life whose reports had first intrigued me about coursing, died suddenly on his way home from a coursing meeting. John succeeded him both on the Life and the Coursing Calendar, the official NCC formbook. John lived in central London near Broadcasting House, and had never learned to drive, so I often picked him up at a station and drove him around the country to meetings. It was good to have some company on long drives between meetings. Sometimes I would stay with him in London and we would catch an early train to somewhere where we had arranged to be picked up by another member of the coursing community.

John later became well known as the betting guru on Channel 4 racing, when he would often use tic-tac signs (not always the right ones!) to accompany his comments on betting movements. He was brilliant at conveying the atmosphere and liveliness of the betting ring to viewers, and would often refer to the ring as the betting jungle. Nowadays it is more like an allotment than a jungle, or even a window-box at the quieter meetings. Some people regarded him as a bit of a buffoon because of the image he cultivated, and there were times when I felt compelled to tell him he was talking nonsense, but in fact he was a skilled, award-winning journalist who uncovered a scheme for after-time betting on greyhound racing, and also Woodrow Wyatt's complicity in doctoring tote dividends.

Travelling in the 1970s before the motorways were all built and other main roads were improved was sometimes exhausting. Dashing back from places like Sandown or Goodwood to the dogs often required some continental driving on the right-hand side of the road and there might even have been the occasional speed limit broken.

I once attended the first day of coursing meeting at Huntingdon, drove back to Bristol for the dogs that night, went home and then drove back to Huntingdon for a 9 am start the next day, and still somehow found time to study the card for that day's coursing. Another time I was at a coursing meeting in Northumberland that was rained off around midday and I drove back to Bristol for the dogs the same evening.

When the weather was favourable I would often cycle to Salisbury, Wincanton or Bath to bet on the rails; I had heard of bookmakers arriving to bet in minor rings by bicycle, but I claim to be the first rails bookmaker to do so. I thus disproved the old saying that you never see a bookie on a bicycle; the other similar saying that you never see a poor bookmaker is true, because once they become poor, they're not bookmakers any more.

Chapter 8

Getting known and rule 4

Because I wasn't very busy at the races in my early days on the rails, I would often choose to go coursing instead. For instance, in November 1977, after betting at Taunton where there were no rails bookmakers but I was now able to bet on the boards in the ring, I missed the Hennessy Gold Cup meeting at Newbury by dashing up to Thirsk where the Old Yorkshire Club had arranged a dinner before the next two days' coursing. This meeting featured an international stake in which eight Irish dogs met eight English dogs; it was held in Yorkshire and County Cork in alternate years, with one Irish and one English dog in each of the opening round's pairings. I arrived too late for dinner, but afterwards there was a callover in which each dog's odds were quoted and diners could back their fancy. Experience had taught me to expect to lay only one dog in each course, which would almost always be the one to win through to the next round, so I was pleasantly surprised to lay all sixteen dogs and to have made a modest profit by the time coursing was over.

I didn't normally lay any ante-post bets, but I was persuaded to lay a couple of regular clients 10/1 and 9/1 about Birds Nest early in that season to win the 1976 Champion Hurdle. Every time he ran I hoped he would run poorly, but all that happened was that his odds shortened with each race that he ran. On the day he was nearly favourite and it was painful to have to take 7/2 to keep the liability affordable. Fortunately, Night Nurse came to the rescue, not to give me a winning race but at least to avert disaster.

After a few years in Devizes, I wanted to move still nearer to Bristol to cut down on the motoring. After looking at a wide variety of places in and around Bristol, in 1976 I eventually settled on a semi-detached house in Larkhall on the eastern side of Bath. By now my father had accepted my choice of career, although it had been far from what he would have chosen for me, and congratulated me on being able to buy my first house – albeit with a mortgage – without parental help. It would amuse him in later years to tell people that his two sons were both accountants, one chartered and one turf. Personally I don't approve of the expression turf accountant, as it is a euphemism and I am not willing to accept that such a thing is required.

I couldn't afford to spend large sums on advertising, but occasionally the opportunity would arise to get my name into the Sporting Life at little or no cost. The first occurred in early 1972 when Gus Dalrymple, a Sporting Life columnist, wrote that, with Hills and Ladbrokes both claiming to be the biggest and greatest, he was sickened by this boasting and he wanted to know who was the smallest and worst. I wrote in – without a stamp of course – to stake my claim, and he came to a point-to-point at Larkhill with me to verify my claim. There he ruled that I wasn't mean enough to qualify for his award, but at least I got my photograph in the Sporting Life!

Another chance came about in late 1975 when Laurie Wyles, an off-course bookmaker who wrote a weekly column in the Sporting Life under the nom-de-plume Michael Rolfe, mentioned a complaint from a punter that he couldn't get a reasonable bet with the public companies' representatives on the rails at Bath. At the time there were proposals to alter the pitch rules in a way that would entrench company bookmakers in the best pitches on the grounds that they were necessary to bolster the market and cater for larger punters. To counter this argument, I wrote to Michael Rolfe to tell him that I had laid £900 to £400 (*2023 equivalent £6,525 to £2,900*), considered a big bet at the time, against the horse in question, which duly got me a mention in a later column.

Getting known and rule 4

The letters pages of the Sporting Life and Racing Post often contained a missive from a member of the racing public that cried out for a reply, not just to get my name in the paper but to make a genuine point. For instance, there was once a letter from a punter who had started a petition for a plan to distribute sleepers' uncollected winnings and wanted help in collecting signatures. I wrote in to say that I was campaigning for the collection of the much larger sum of unpaid punters' losses, and would be grateful to anyone who could help collect signatures – on cheques.

A frequent topic in letters pages was rule 4 deductions after the withdrawal of a horse from a race. The system of adjusting odds to compensate for the absence of a non-runner, on which stakes are returned, is laid down by the Tattersalls Committee. This is a committee set up in 1886 comprising bookmakers and other betting experts to settle betting disputes and draw up rules to cover various aspects of betting on horseracing; their rule 4 specifies a scale of deductions from winnings only, based solely on the odds of the withdrawn horse. The rule has had minor adjustments over the years, but it remains fundamentally flawed, as it should stipulate a scale of deductions, usually smaller than in the existing scale, to returns including stake. There are, however, cases, especially in the 6/1 to 10/1 range, where the deduction would be inadequate even if applied to returns instead of just winnings, such as in the example below. Ideally the deduction should also take into account the odds of all the other runners, which would have been impractical without computers when the rule was instituted, but less so now. When I was invited to appear before the Committee to try to explain why I thought the rule is flawed, I just saw blank faces, even though I was talking to a group of supposed experts on betting, and I thought I would have had more success trying to explain Einstein's relativity theories.

The rule works reasonably well in the majority of races, though always in favour of the punter, but throws up huge anomalies when there is a short-priced favourite or few runners. There are frequent cases where a withdrawal showed up how inadequate the deduction is, but of course it is not necessary to have an actual withdrawal to demonstrate the consequence of the flawed rule. An example of how unfairly the rule can operate occurred at Ascot in March 1990 when Barney Curley, renowned punter and owner/trainer, withdrew his horse Ardbrin not long before the off as one of his many protests about something or other.

At the time of withdrawal I had taken twelve bets on winning favourite Jubail, and after a bit of hedging they added up to liabilities on that horse of £18,408 to £14,760 staked. I had taken just two bets, now void, on Ardbrin totalling £192 at 6/1, and its withdrawal meant a deduction on winnings of 10% in accordance with the prescribed scale. This amounted in total to £1,840, but mathematically the deduction should have been about 14% from returns, i.e. £4,643. Barney was fined £1,000 for breaking the rule about withdrawing a fit horse, but I was effectively 'fined' more than twice as much for abiding by a flawed rule, as I lost that much more than I would have done if his horse had run. I also lost the chance of Ardbrin winning, though Barney would presumably not have withdrawn it unless he thought, or knew, that it would not win.

Another topic that cropped up was the issue of reducing ante-post odds when the same horse was backed to win two different races, instead of laying the full multiplied odds for each individual race. In 1971 a northern bookmaker wrote to say that this was not mathematically justified, and I replied to try to explain why it was. Phil Bull, founder of Timeform, also had something of a blind spot on this issue, which I thought was surprising for someone of such an analytical intellect; he later had an account with me, but I never got the chance to discuss the matter with him. The hypothetical scenario I use to illustrate the point is as follows.

Two greyhounds are to run two match races over a straight course a week apart in trap 1 and trap 6; one is a top open race dog, the other is a bottom-graded runner. The trap draw is to be made ten minutes before the first match race, and will apply for both races; there is no possibility of any corrupt practice occurring (for any cynics – I said it was hypothetical!). As no one knows which dog is in which trap, the odds for each race are 10-11 each of two, but if anyone was silly enough to lay full multiplied odds for a double, you could back the 1 and 1 double at over 5/2 and the 6 and 6 double at over 5/2 and be assured of a tidy profit when the better dog won both times, as would be almost certain.

The question of how much any reduction should be, for instance for a horse to win both 2000 Guineas and Derby, is a different argument. There are cases where the multiplied odds should be increased, such as when a horse is quoted for two different Cheltenham races before its target race is known, as it is very unlikely that it will even run in both races, but the point I was making was that it was wrong to say there was never any justification for laying less than full multiplied odds.

I did occasionally have paid advertisements for prices for coursing meetings, and later on the Racing Post had a daily space detailing where several bookmakers would be operating, with each bookmaker paying a small sum to cover the cost of the space. In time, several dropped out of this arrangement, often leaving me as the only bookmaker listed, but still paying the same sum, which made it good-value advertising. It was flattering to be told by some punters that they sometimes based their decision of which meeting to attend on my choice of attendance, and well-known punter Simon 'Dodger' McCartney even suggested in a letter to the Racing Post that racecourses should pay me appearance money; unfortunately this idea was not adopted.

Chapter 9

Cyril Stein, other leading bookmakers, and keeping warm

I had worked for other bookmakers at the Derby before, but the first Derby where I stood on the rails in my own name was Empery's Derby in 1976. I had just missed one of the biggest Derby upsets when Snow Knight won at 50/1 in 1975 and I lost on the Derby itself, as I did on nearly every Derby subsequently, though not on the day. One year even a blind man backed three winners with me, which made me think it was going to be really hard for me to win there. But my main memory of Empery's Derby was that of Cyril Stein, head of my former employer Ladbrokes, having £50 each way on the winner. I sent him a cheque at the end of the week, but a few days later I received a call complaining that I had paid only the standard ⅕ the odds for the place part instead of the ¼ that some bookmakers were offering on the race. He must have thought it beneath his dignity to ring me himself, so he had instructed a minion to do so. I said that there was no reason for Mr Stein to assume that I was offering any concessionary place rate but the minion, in a presumably instructed attempt to shame me into paying another £25, said that all the big bookmakers were paying ¼ the odds a place. I replied that I was only a Little bookmaker and I heard no more about it.

I had another run-in with Cyril Stein on Derby day some years later in 1983. A month or so earlier he had had a bet or two for which I sent him a bill for around £600. Having received no cheque, I sent him an account rendered, but with still no reply. So on Derby day

Cyril Stein, other leading bookmakers, and keeping warm

I told him that I had already sent him two accounts, and that I hoped I would not need to send him another. He huffed and puffed, gathered the cash from his men on the Ladbrokes pitch, came over to my pitch and almost threw the money at me, calling me what the Sporting Life reported as 'a most unbookmaker-like phrase'. I should have said that even if I was a spiv, which I believe was the term he used, at least I pay my debts promptly, but I just mumbled thank you. The next time he asked me for a bet I told him he would have to pay on with cash, which he declined to do. I always liked to tease him when he came racing by calling out 'cash bets taken' when he came near my pitch. When John Banks named one of his horses Adorable Cyril, I don't think anyone inferred that John – or anyone else – really did adore Cyril. When he was more active in running Ladbrokes in earlier decades, there was a saying that if you could get a bet on with Ladbrokes, you didn't want to be on!

My meetings with the other leaders of the 'big three' bookmakers were more amicable. At Newmarket races one day in the late 1960s I asked William Hill to sign a petition being organised in support of coursing, which, having been a leading coursing bookmaker, especially after the Second World War, he readily agreed to do. A man of imposing presence, he had served in the Black and Tans during the Irish War of Independence and subsequently made his name betting on pony racing and trotting at courses such as Northolt Park and Hawthorn Hill before the war. He was declared unfit to serve in the war and bet on the rails at most wartime meetings, continuing to do so after the war. He is often revered as the most daring and skilled bookmaker of the twentieth century, a description he doubtless deserves, but my admiration for him received a severe jolt when I read his biography, William Hill, the Man & the Business. This suggests that in his early days he did not always settle his liabilities, and that later when the formidable and high-staking punter Dorothy Paget was betting with him, her jockey was riding more for William Hill than for Dorothy Paget.

I was sometimes asked if I intended to be the second William Hill, to which I always replied 'No, I am going to be the first Stephen Little'. When I read in his biography about jockeys and brown envelopes, I was glad I hadn't been another William Hill, as I can hold my head up and say that I never got involved in such dealings, in spite of a few approaches. William Hill suddenly stopped betting on the racecourse at Royal Ascot in 1955, reputedly in frustration at the decline in the strength of the racecourse market. What would he have made of the state of that market now? He eventually died of a heart attack in the Rutland Arms in Newmarket in 1971 at the age of 68.

I knew his much younger brother Joe Ward Hill as he frequently came to coursing meetings, especially at Huntingdon which he sometimes sponsored. He also ran greyhounds, who bore the prefix Lynwood in their names. Rather than joining his brother's business, he had preferred to plough his own furrow, building up a chain of betting shops in several towns in and around Stevenage in Hertfordshire and at one time had a few rails pitches.

I met Bob Green of Mecca bookmakers when he came to a bookmakers' meeting to tell us about the proposed SIS service to relay pictures of races to betting shops instead of the Extel commentaries. I was not impressed when, in response to a comment that it would severely affect racecourse attendances, his reply was that it didn't matter because greyhound meetings supplying the BAGS (Bookmakers' Afternoon Greyhound Service) often had sparse attendances but still provided a service for betting shops.

My meeting with Joe Coral was at the Victoria Club, which was a club for bookmakers where the Victoria Casino is now situated off Edgware Road in London. I was not a member myself as I was not well established at that time. In the days when there were many more strong independent bookmakers than now, they used to hold callovers on big races, where members would offer odds against each runner in turn and bet among themselves; they would be reported in the Sporting Life, with details of what prices were offered and laid, and would form the basis of ante-post markets. The Club held an annual snooker tournament, with all the members sat around the table betting in running, even on individual shots. I cannot imagine anything more off-putting than cueing up for a pot and hearing someone call out 'take 5/2 that he pots this'!

Joe Coral, born as Joe Kagalitsky in Warsaw, Poland, had come to England with his widowed mother as a boy before the First World War. In contrast to William Hill, he was a slight man, not much taller than five foot, who had suffered from polio in his youth, but started by taking and standing bets from work colleagues before his career took off with the advent of greyhound racing, with pitches at White City, Harringay, Clapton and Walthamstow dog tracks and later credit and street betting. It is believed that he was the first bookmaker to take bets in London on the individual courses of the Waterloo Cup, and won £5,000 on the 1944 Cup. He always wore a bowler hat and coined his slogan 'Never a quarrel, bet with Coral'. His business gradually expanded into the firm that still bears his name today. Little did I imagine then that I would later represent that firm on racecourses after the upheaval in pitch administration still to come, by which time Joe Coral had died a few years previously.

The latter years of the 1970s were a period of gradual progress. Having survived the first few years on the rails, my confidence and ambition remained intact, but I still needed to build a clientele of regular customers, both credit and cash. I would still clerk for myself on the quieter days, and usually found no difficulty in fitting all the day's business on one page of the clerking book. However, one symptom of things proceeding in the right direction was that in the middle of the 1970s, I had progressed from driving a patched-up Austin Cambridge to a Mercedes, even though it was an umpteenth-hand model, and by 1979 had upgraded to a Mercedes 250.

I applied for a few more pitches and started betting at Wolverhampton and Ludlow in 1977, York in 1978 and Liverpool, now Aintree, in 1979. I had also risen well up the waiting lists for Tattersalls pitches at Wincanton and Taunton, which meant that I could bet there if there were a few pitch holders absent. One of the largest bets I laid in this period was £9,000 to £1,000 *(£41,400 to £4,600)* against Son Fils at Ascot in 1978 on the Heath day, which at that time followed the four days of Royal Ascot on the Saturday. I hedged most of it, it lost, but I still lost on the race, after which I sped off to the evening meeting at Warwick.

At this time I was still regularly going to Bristol dogs at Eastville after racing in the afternoon. Relaxation of laws restricting the number of meetings at dog tracks meant there were often three meetings a week to go to, and driving west with the sun in my eyes, barely time to eat anything other than a snatched meal on the way, and not getting home until gone ten at night was getting wearisome. On Bank Holidays there was racing there in the morning, Chepstow in the afternoon and back to Eastville in the evening. There was always a queue of traffic to cross over the Severn Bridge, and from there to the racecourse, so I and other Eastville bookmakers heading for Chepstow needed to judge how many races we had to miss to get there in time. One day I was sitting in traffic on the approach to Chepstow when I was starting to panic about whether I would reach the course in time for the first race. I felt I had no option but to drive a little way down the cycle path on the other side of the road into the town and avoid the traffic that way. What I didn't know was that the driver of the car in the queue behind me was an off-duty policewoman, so in due course I was summoned to Chepstow police station to explain myself. I was very tempted to say 'Yes, I know the sign said Cyclists Only, but I'm a cyclist, so I thought I was entitled to go there', but considered it wiser to hold my tongue. Although I was formally interviewed, eventually they took no action.

I am constantly amazed by how many people still remark on the fur coat I used to wear, or ask where it is. The first one I bought, in the late 1970s, was a musquash coat from a furrier in the West End of London. I really felt the cold when I stood out all day in icy winds,

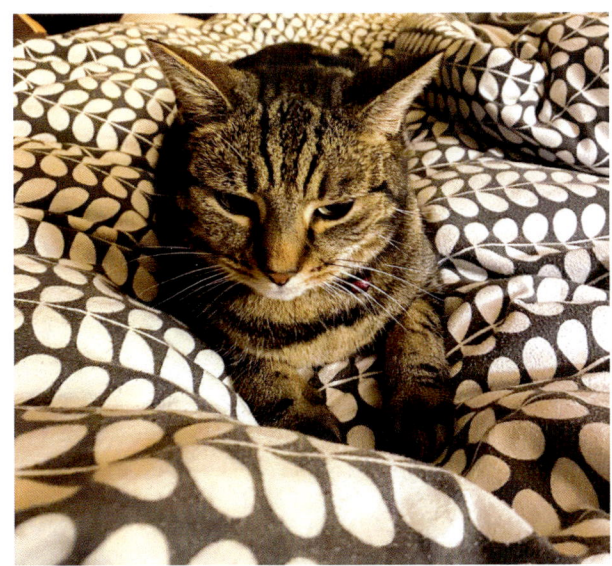

Alfie; a feline celebrity in his street in Bath.

With grandparents Annetta and William Crawford, and Alice Little at Mill Hill.

Father leading Judges' Procession, Lincoln Assizes.

Above left: Father and Mother in the mid 1970's at Meonstoke Vicarage, Hampshire, his last parish before retiring.

Above right: Great-great grandfather James Alexander Crawford judging at the Calcutta races.

Above left: Father and sister at our cousin's wedding to the future Bishop of Carlisle.

Above right: Plaid brooch with family motto.

Aerial view of the vicarage at Skellingthorpe, set in nine acres.

Above: St Lawrences' church in Skellingthorpe where I sang in the choir.

Right: Interior of former St Ann's church, Nottingham.

Above left: With Alex Smith, John McCririck and Johanna Williams at a Newmarket coursing meeting in 1981.

Above right: Presenting the 1993 Waterloo Cup to Brian Divilly, subsequently President of the Irish Coursing Club, after the victory of his Crafty Tessie.

Above: Cheltenham Festival cards, 1991.

Left: Bicycle and Bentley.

Above left: Helping out at Cheltenham, March 2023.

Above right: First meeting attended, Lincoln, 1960.

Above left: Shouting the odds at Chepstow with John Durston clerking.

Above right: With assistant Ashley Woodford at the Waterloo Cup in 1993.

Above left: At a point-to-point at Larkhill in 1972.

Above right: Card for Frankie Dettori's Malevolent Seven, September 1996.

On the Rails at Bath.

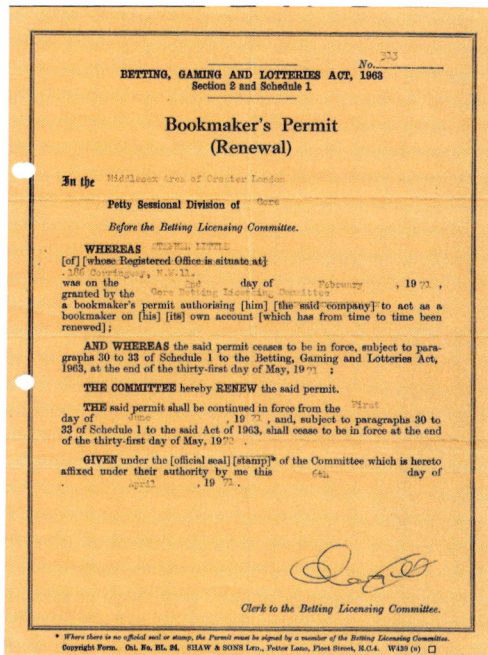 

Above left: First permit, February 1971.

Above right: Ring joint.

Below left: Youth Hostel Association membership card.

Below right: Thomas Henry Dey, 1876-1932.

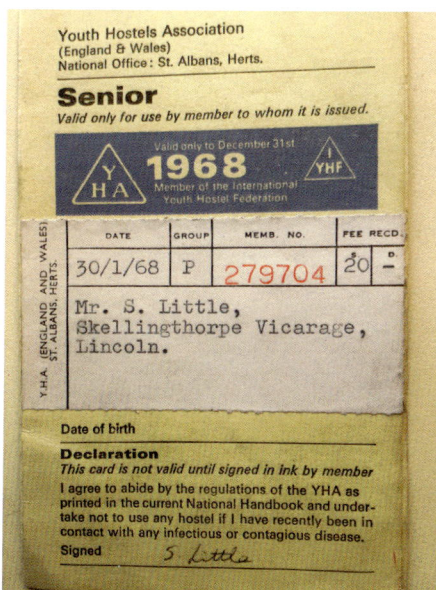 

Geraldine Rees, myself and Sir Mark Prescott, Bt at Clonmel Coursing Festival, 2023.

Hollow Tree and Harriet Glen at Les Landes, Jersey.

and a fur coat is much more effective than any cloth coat, and much lighter than a sheepskin coat. I felt a bit self-conscious about wearing it at first, but I thought it was worth it if it kept me warm – which it did. I didn't realise that it would become almost a trademark. My mother (yes, bookmakers do have mothers!) was astounded once when she was watching Cheltenham on TV and between races the screen was showing a general crowd shot with thousands of racegoers; Richard Pitman, surveying the scene, said ' … and there's Stephen Little in his fur coat …'. At a later, very wet Cheltenham, that coat got so wet through that it never recovered, and I bought another similar coat in a second-hand clothes shop in Newmarket.

This one lasted for several years until one mild winter when I didn't wear it at all, and when I wanted to wear it the following winter, it was riddled with moths whose grubs had devoured much of the fur, leaving bald patches. Fur coats should be put in cold storage when out of use for any length of time, but I had neglected the New Testament advice 'lay not up for yourselves treasures upon earth where moth and rust doth corrupt'. Since then I have tried to find a musquash or similar coat large enough to fit me, but meanwhile I occasionally wear a bearskin coat when it's cold enough. I like to claim that I strangled it myself, but no one seems to believe me.

Chapter 10

Owning horses and dogs, night in a police cell, breathalysed, and backgammon

Owning a racehorse had never been a particular ambition of mine, but in 1978 circumstances conspired to lead to joining the ranks of owners. Harriet Glen, a sculptress and equine artist specialising in making jewellery, had been champion lady rider in Australia two years running and was now living in Newmarket harbouring an ambition to ride a winner, or preferably more, in Europe. We agreed to buy a horse in equal partnership, and at a Newmarket sale in December we bought Hollow Tree, a lightly raced 3-year-old mare by Wolver Hollow, who had been trained by Jeremy Tree, for 2,500 guineas and sent her to Toby Balding, training at Weyhill near Andover.

She ran several times the next year in England at various minor courses, and on August Bank Holiday I travelled on the ferry from Weymouth to Jersey, arriving early in a very wet morning. Hollow Tree was running in the Jersey Vase (not to be confused with Royal Ascot's Jersey Stakes!) and Harriet rode her to victory. I didn't back her, mainly because the few bookmakers standing at the Les Landes course were shamelessly betting to such a huge percentage that there was clearly no value in doing so, but it was still a great pleasure to see the two of them sweep up the straight to mission accomplished. Hollow Tree returned to the sales in October, where I put in a few bids with a view to keeping her as sole owner, but she was sold for 3,000 guineas to go to India, where she bred three winners by Home Run and died in 1994. Buying for 2,500 guineas and selling for 3,000 guineas might sound like a useful profit, but the associated expenses of transport, sales commission, etc. whittled it down to around £50.

Although I enjoyed the more direct involvement in racing, and am glad I had that experience, I have resisted any urge to dabble in racehorse ownership since, as I feel it's a bit like taking 6/4 about a 10/1 chance. Taking 7/1 or 8/1 might have been acceptable for the fun of it, but I couldn't convince myself that the chances of avoiding spending large amounts with minimal return would be in my favour. I never harboured thoughts of emulating William Hill, who became heavily involved in both owning and breeding thoroughbreds; apart from some of his early practices being somewhat dubious, as outlined in his biography, much of his fortune was derived from off-course postal and telephone betting, and later from betting shops, after initial reluctance when they were legalised in 1961. He and the other bookmakers who became well known also had the advantage of operating in what was probably the best time to be a bookmaker, namely just after the Second World War when there was plenty of money around, not much to spend it on, and betting was almost exclusively on horses and greyhounds. I wanted to concentrate on the racecourse, so I never wished to branch out into off-course betting. I felt that having to supervise an office, or offices, and worry about what was happening elsewhere while I was on course, would spoil my enjoyment of going racing.

Owning coursing greyhounds was more like taking 6/4 about a 1,000/1 chance, but at least it was cheaper, and I had already joined the ranks of coursing owners. Many owners had systems of naming their dogs, usually with a prefix, which could be registered for exclusive use, or using names with their own initials – I chose the latter method. I thought that Seldom Led would be an appropriate name for a dog that I hoped would live up to its name, but someone else had already had the same idea and won the Greyhound Derby at White City in 1931, so that was unavailable. I applied for Sporting Life, but was told that advertising names were not allowed. I protested that there were dogs named Black Boots and White Mercedes at the time, but to no avail. Salic Law was a law which some countries once had prohibiting having a female monarch, so I thought that was a suitable name, being a confirmed bachelor at that time. Next was Sine Labe, who won a couple of stakes at minor meetings around 1980. My great-great-great grandfather James Henry Crawford had adopted, or perhaps appropriated, the motto 'Sine Labe Nota', which was the motto of one branch of the Crawford clan; it translates as 'Mark without stain' or 'Distinction without disgrace', which I hope I have lived up to.

The coursing season would run from late September to early March, and in the close season, some of the dogs I owned would also run on the track, usually in graded races. Most were trained by coursing judge Ronnie Mills at Gloucester, now closed like many of the other tracks in the west, such as Cardiff, Taunton, Trowbridge, Yeovil and other independents (i.e. licensed, but not under NGRC rules, known as flapping tracks). I was less interested in going to see them run at the track, as I regarded coursing as 'the real thing', where greyhounds perform as nature intended, testing all the attributes that greyhounds have been bred over the centuries to excel at, including not only speed but also agility, determination and stamina – whereas greyhound racing is comparatively artificial.

Coursing meetings were usually held on a farm well off the beaten track and not generally accessible by public transport, so usually car was the only practical means of getting there. Occasionally I would leave the car at home and travel by train; coursing people were often very accommodating in giving me lifts to or from the nearest station, even if it meant sitting on the straw in the back of a dog van. One such occasion was the only time I have spent a night in a police cell. A meeting at Huntingdon was followed the next day by one at

Scottish National, held on a large estate near Annan. I travelled by train after the meeting at Huntingdon to Carlisle, where I thought it would be easy to find somewhere to stay, and when I arrived late in the evening I tried a few places that were either closed or full. I asked at the police station where I was likely to find somewhere, and they very kindly drove me round to a few hotels to try, but they were also fully booked. Fortunately for me there was not much crime in Carlisle that night, so they allowed me to stay in one of their empty cells. It wasn't comfortable, but at least the door wasn't locked and I was free to walk out whenever I wished. In fact, I walked out earlier than I wished, as they said I had to leave at 6 am when the shift changed, so I got an early train to Annan where I found somewhere to have breakfast and secure a lift the few miles to the coursing ground.

In 1981, Bristol Greyhound Stadium was awarded a BAGS contract, meaning that they would hold all their meetings in the afternoon for the benefit of betting shops, with few punters in attendance, instead of in the evening. I therefore had to decide whether to continue there or just stick to horseracing and coursing. It didn't take long to decide, as I was getting busier, with more regular clients, at the races and the 4% tax on the horseracing turnover in the afternoon would often be more than the total greyhound turnover in the evening. Profitability had been very volatile; there were periods when dogs that had been backed were the only runners involved in the race – then there would be a spell when what happened in the race bore no relation to what had happened in the betting. As a sport I much preferred horseracing to dog racing, and now I had more flexibility to attend more racing and coursing fixtures.

In the early 1980s turnover started to increase, but only gradually. One race that sticks in the mind from that period was the 1981 Triumph Hurdle. With bets sometimes coming thick and fast in the cauldron that is the Cheltenham Festival betting market, it is not always as easy to control liabilities as at quieter meetings, and I was standing Broadsword for what at the time was too much. It led over the last hurdle and though I couldn't see very well from my pitch I feared the worst, but all of a sudden Baron Blakeney, a 66/1 chance trained by the then relatively unknown trainer Martin Pipe, got up to pass the post in front, to the great relief of many bookmakers, including me.

I was now starting to attract business from more and larger punters, including some owners and trainers, and I never minded taking trade money, if they wanted to take the prices I was offering. Some off-course bookmakers were very active in the course market, because most off-course bets were at starting price, which was then determined solely by the prices on the racecourse. Ladbrokes and Hills were the main on-course hedgers, and there were also some bets sent by other bookmakers who did not have their own men on course via the blower. This practice often attracted criticism of manipulating the market, which was not fair comment; ensuring a 6/4 chance isn't returned at 5/2 is more like correcting a market anomaly. This raises the question 'Who says it's a 6/4 chance?', to which the answer is the volume of punters who have backed it in the offices.

Turnover was increasing, not only at the big Cheltenham and Ascot meetings but also at courses such as Newbury, Salisbury and Bath, though I would still clerk for myself at some lesser meetings without being rushed off my feet. I felt I had to go to as many meetings as possible to be seen, so coursing had to take a back seat. I didn't want to see betting disappear from the smaller coursing meetings, but fortunately a prominent coursing owner, Alex Smith from Great Yarmouth, who won more than his share of coursing trophies, held a bookmaker's licence and stepped into the breach. I wouldn't have missed betting at the Waterloo Cup though, but it rarely clashed with any of my meetings anyway, and I still went coursing when I was free to do so, but didn't make a book when there was clearly not enough potential business for two bookmakers.

By 1982 business had improved enough to enable another change of address. I moved to my next house in September 1982; it was still a semi-detached, and still with a mortgage, but it was larger and nearer to the centre of Bath, a Victorian house near Royal Victoria Park. And transport was upgraded when I acquired a Rolls-Royce Silver Shadow in 1983.

I also dipped my toe into race sponsorship. My first attempt was a handicap chase at Wincanton in September 1983, which attracted only six runners. My race was the fourth race on the card, but the meeting was abandoned after the third race, as some horses had been slipping on the bends. Someone suggested that I had sprinkled silicone on the course so that I wouldn't be called upon to provide my contribution to the prize money! The next attempt was more successful, a handicap hurdle with twenty-two runners in January 1984, won by the well-backed Stans Pride, making the betting on the race even more costly than the sponsorship.

Many credit bookmakers wooed their customers by throwing lavish parties and sending gifts such as cigars, wine or even just diaries at Christmas, but I did not, saying that my generosity extended throughout the year, with no extras at Christmas. However, I did often enjoy joining other racegoers for dinner, attending racing functions and spending time socialising in the bar after racing when I was not travelling with the staff. My paternal grandfather, who I never knew, had not been averse to drinking, and is said to have 'signed the pledge' – several times! – but I had never got the taste for alcohol, even after sampling various forms. I have probably spent more time in bars than most non-drinkers, which once led to my being breathalysed when driving away from Wincanton. I may have been doing 31 mph when I was stopped and told 'blow into this please'. My only worry was that the device might be faulty, and the policeman kept saying 'blow harder' as he was surprised to see a zero reading. After he accepted that zero was indeed correct, I asked him why he had thought to breathalyse me, to which he replied that he thought he had smelt alcohol; I can only assume that my coat in the back of the car had absorbed some fumes while I was in the racecourse bar.

I had learned to play the board game backgammon some years previously, and often played in a club in London when I was there, as well as regularly in Bristol. I was far from a top player, but being a dice game, the mixture of skill and luck means that if a reasonably competent player takes on a champion, they may be odds against, but, especially in a short match, they have a realistic chance of winning, unlike if the game was chess or tennis for instance. Just as some punters think that when they win they are geniuses with the form book and when they lose the jockey and/or trainer went crooked, it is always tempting to think that a win is the result of expert play and a loss is down to sheer bad luck with the dice.

The highlight of my backgammon career was winning an international tournament in Valencia, Spain, in December 1981. Victory needed a whole series of flukes: I hadn't planned to go, but Cheltenham that weekend was frozen off, so I and a backgammon pal, Martin Reade, decided to head for Valencia. The weather was so bad that nearly all flights out of Heathrow were cancelled; we caught the last flight to Paris before Heathrow shut down, and took an overnight train from Paris to Valencia. Instead of entering the novices division as I usually did, I entered the main event, for which two recent world champions were also entered; there were thirty-three runners and they were drawn together to play the only extra round, so that was one danger about to go out immediately. I won my first three rounds against local players, then was drawn to meet a quality player who had recently won a good tournament at Aspinalls Club in London, but I beat him by taking a few chances that came off.

Now I was in the final, which Martin had also reached in the other half of the draw. He was a better player than me, but the dice went my way and I won the tournament! Currency restrictions were particularly tight at the time and I had to fly home, with the weather having eased, with about 250,000 pesetas in my underwear. I also had a fine Lladro china trophy, but fortunately that didn't have to be secreted on my person, as trophies won in international competition are not subject to customs duty. There was a group of players in London who went to most such tournaments in Europe but had swerved Valencia; once they heard I had won there, they all went the following year, reasoning that if I could win, anyone could.

When in London I would also sometimes visit casinos, though I found watching other people play more appealing than playing myself. I would occasionally get sucked into playing blackjack or craps, but if I had had a good winning day at the races and then lost £100 in a casino I would be furious with myself. One evening in Aspinalls Club off Sloane Street I watched Australian tycoon Kerry Packer playing blackjack; he had a stack of chips as big as saucers in front of him, each marked £500, and had the table to himself, betting on every box. I was confused about how he was being paid when he was dealt a blackjack (ace and court card, which paid 6/4 instead of evens), until I realised that each £500 chip actually represented £5,000! He never accepted the mandatory insurance offer before the deal continued, saying that he didn't want to take 2/1 about a 9/4 chance. He played for some time, with John Aspinall himself observing intently, occasionally signing a chit for more chips, but I don't know whether he won or lost on the session.

The Bristol casino where I used to play eventually closed down, and for several years I knew of nowhere to play, until I heard of a club in Bristol that met twice a week, which is where I mostly play now. Nowadays there are computer programs that can analyse matches, or particular positions or moves, to the nth degree, and moves that were thought to be good or bad years ago have been shown to be not as good or bad as previously thought. Computers cannot be consulted during play, but some players record their matches, or photograph a position on the board to analyse later, and while I was a long way from being a top player before anyway, I feel that I have been rather left behind in the computer age.

Chapter 11

Computers and mobile phones

For most racecourse bookmakers, their work is done by the time they leave the racecourse, but a rails bookmaker needs regular customers who have accounts, which involves sending out statements at regular intervals. As I had no office, I dealt with that part of the business myself, sending out handwritten accounts on printed forms each week. I always tried to get this job done on Saturday evening and get everything in the post as soon as possible. One week I had been a little too hasty; someone backed a horse in a race in America and when I listened to the race on the radio and heard it didn't win, I finalised the accounts and sent them all off. A few days later the phone rang with a complaint that I had settled a winner as a loser; it transpired that the horse the punter had backed was coupled with the winner, turning a losing account into a winning one, so I had to apologise and send him a cheque.

When I began, manually was the only way to do it, but as technology advanced and became more portable and affordable, the process gradually became more mechanised. The first step was a pocket-sized computer that could be mounted on a small printer, by which means I could enter all the credit bets, sort them for each punter and print small slips to be stuck onto the accounts to be posted at the end of the week. I also had a rather primitive machine that could transfer addresses from a set of cards onto envelopes.

I was always searching for ways both to reduce and speed up the workload, and to improve the appearance of what I was sending out, and in 1984 I was recommended by my backgammon comrade Martin

Computers and mobile phones

Reade to look at a Husky computer. On investigation it seemed ideal; it was about the size of a modern-day tablet, but much thicker and heavier, and waterproof and shockproof so that it could be taken to the races without any worries about rain or being dropped. I bought one and set about programming it for my particular purpose. One day I was doing some programming on a train when who should sit opposite me but the managing director of Husky Computers. We chatted about how I intended to use one of his computers, and he said he always liked to publicise the different uses for them, which led to a story, with a photo of me at Warwick using my computer, in the Bath & West Evening Chronicle on April 1985 – more free publicity!

I was then able to input all the bets from the field book, including cash bets, and it would verify the clerk's profit or loss figures, tell me how much cash I should have (if any!), print daily and weekly figures including the long list of accounts still to be settled, and at the end of the week print the statements ready to be sent out. It also stored every client's address, in highly abbreviated form, so that I could print address labels, and later directly onto envelopes when I acquired a specialist printer. On quiet days I could enter the bets race by race, and all would be balanced up before I reached home. At one period there was a postbox nearby that had a collection on Sundays, and punters were impressed that they could back a winner on Saturday and receive the cheque on Monday morning.

As I got busier, the process of writing all the cheques, as well as being painful, was getting more tedious and time-consuming. I persuaded my bank to accept cheques for payment with a printed signature made up of dots, which did bear some resemblance to my written signature. Next, I set to work on programming the computer to print cheques with the date, amount and signature, and the amount translated into words all in the right place. All went smoothly until the first time I had to send a cheque for more than £100,000 to J.P. McManus. A few days later his brother Kevin rang to say that they had received my cheque, but that the words of the amount had become garbled and would be rejected when paid in. I had programmed the computer to translate sums below £100,000 correctly, but had not allowed for six-figure sums! I made a grovelling apology, sent him another cheque, handwritten this time, and updated the program.

Although often hard work and frustrating, I did enjoy the programming as an intellectual challenge. 100% accuracy is needed, as even the NASA space programme found once when something went wrong because there was a full stop where a comma should have been. The frustration felt when a piece of code doesn't do what is expected is compensated by the sense of satisfaction when it does eventually do what is wanted. When I was in the Beresford & Smith office, all accounts were handwritten, but by now most if not all office bookmakers would have computerised their systems, though I was probably the first racecourse-only bookmaker to use a computer in his business.

I put my programming experience to greater use when I collaborated with Johanna Williams, who had been Sir Mark Prescott's racing secretary, to create a program to help trainers with their entries. Each week trainers would receive the Racing Calendar from Weatherby's with details and entry forms for all races coming up three weeks later. The original concept was that trainers' office staff could put the details, including their form, of each of their horses, such as age, preferred distance, and type and value of race, etc. into their own computer and would be sent a disk with all the details of the races for the week. The program could then print the week's races with just the names of each of the trainer's horses that might be suitable under each race so that the selection of horses to enter in each race was easier.

The program for inputting races had to enable all details such as distance, eligibility criteria, penalties and allowances, and other incidental information, to be entered as quickly and accurately as possible. We soon learned how to cope with the many variations such as auction races, but there was still the occasional condition, such as in military races or depending on the sire's racing record, that defied the computer's ability to check, so they had to be marked as requiring manual checking. The program for trainers' offices also had to permit a wealth of detail to be entered easily. Our first customer was Richard Hannon (senior), one of the Queen's trainers, and in time many of the other top trainers, both flat and National Hunt, became subscribers. We named the system Easy-Entry, and it was gratifying sometimes to see in adverts for trainers' office staff that experience with Easy-Entry was an asset.

Over time the system expanded to include the recording of other information for trainers, such as blood test and vaccination records, with due dates for future vaccinations, and the programme book covering many months, including foreign races, so that trainers could plan ahead for their better horses. Then five-day entry came along, which required a major overhaul of the system.

The programming language I used was MSbasic, which compared to modern computing language was like programming in Sanskrit. Its limitations became apparent as the amount of racing expanded and the programs frequently had to be adjusted to allow for ever more races each week. Eventually it had to be rewritten in a more modern language, and although I looked at using Visual Basic, I soon realised that I wouldn't have time both to learn the new language and update the program, so that task had to be passed elsewhere. Writing the original program had coincided with a cold winter with much racing cancelled, and I saw enough of Visual Basic to see how much easier it would have been if only that had been available at the time.

By now I was using a small voice recorder during betting, which helped to resolve any query or dispute that occasionally arose. But a much more significant technological advance was the advent of mobile telephones in 1985. Before this, if an office bookmaker wanted to hedge a bet into the racecourse market and didn't have his own men at the course, he would have to use the Victoria Blower service, whereby he could ring their office for a message to be sent to a particular bookmaker or for the blower staff to place bets as best they could. Now the off-course bookmaker could speak directly to a bookmaker on course and ask him for a price and place a bet or ask him to put it on.

Off-course bets were subject to 8% turnover tax and Betting Levy, but on-course bets were taxed at 4%, and course bookmakers paid only a fixed Levy charge annually. To qualify for the lower rate, both backer and bookmaker had to be at the course, but if a course bookmaker accepted a bet from an off-course bookmaker as a business transaction, that was also treated as an on-course bet. Customs & Excise officials were wary that course bookmakers would be accepting phone bets from their own clients and passing them off as on-course bets, which led to a lot of wrangling about how this would be regulated. I pointed out that any bookmaker who was willing, as I was, to share his phone records with C&E would thus be able to prove that he was acting within the rules. It was eventually agreed that we could take bets by phone from off-course bookmakers if several conditions were met: each such bet had to be marked with a T in the book; bookmakers had to supply their betting duty number; bookmakers outside the UK had to write at least annually to confirm that they were licensed bookmakers and that all their bets were business hedging bets. Other punters could ring for a bet if they were at the same course, but I made it clear that if they intended to do that, if for instance they were some way from the rails in a box high up in the stand, they had to let me know they were there beforehand.

Once several course bookmakers had started using phones, I compiled a list of phone users at each racecourse under the heading Course Direct, which I circulated to as many office bookmakers as I could find, in the hope that it would encourage them to think of the racecourse market first as the best place to hedge. I made no charge to anyone who wished to be added to the list, or who received it, as I considered that the effort was worthwhile as a means of strengthening course markets. Every course had at least one phone user, with most courses having several.

Computers and mobile phones

For reasons I could never fathom, racecourses felt justified in charging bookmakers who used a phone an extra £15 for doing so, even though they made no contribution to making them work, either financial or physical. By law, courses could only charge five times the admission to the ring they were operating in, so I saw this as a dangerous precedent if bookmakers meekly accepted the charge without objection. Would they charge us for bringing an umbrella? Or for wearing an overcoat? I believe that if our associations had challenged the legality of the £15 supplement, it would have been easy to show that it could not be justified, but without any support from other bookmakers, it would prove difficult for my one-man protest to have any effect. I once happened to meet Stanley Jackson, then chief executive of the Racecourse Association, on a train and I realised afterwards that I should have asked him if he had bought a ticket for his phone, and if not why not. I was disappointed that no one else supported my stand against the imposition of the £15 phone charge, but I saw no option but to grit my teeth and pay, albeit without a smile.

Chapter 12

Increasing turnover and a new Bentley

In the mid-1980s turnover continued to increase steadily, aided by the trade turnover on the mobile phone. I was gradually attracting more high-staking punters, and as the way I was operating seemed to be working, that emboldened me to take larger bets, which in turn pushed me into laying more on other horses to balance them. I found the phone to be a very useful aid to increasing turnover, and that even the quietest raceday could suddenly come to life when the phone rang.

An even bigger fillip to turnover than the mobile phone was the end of the 4% on-course betting tax, announced during the Cheltenham Festival in the budget of March 1987. Annual turnover, which is takings less sums hedged, rose by around 30% from 1986 to 1987, by a further 50% in 1988, and by a further 50% in 1989; profit did increase, but unfortunately not by anything like the same rate. How true it is that turnover is vanity, profit is sanity!

Attending two horseracing meetings in one day was something I and my team did quite often in summer when it was feasible. In June 1989 in the week before Royal Ascot we went to six meetings in three days – Newbury and Kempton on Wednesday, Newbury and Chepstow on Thursday, and Sandown and Goodwood on Friday. As many a bookmaker, jockey and trainer has found, constantly travelling up and down and across the country can be tiring, but I felt that if I wanted to serve clients to my best ability, I needed to be there to do so.

Increasing turnover and a new Bentley

By 1988 I was taking a few five-figure bets at Cheltenham and Royal Ascot, and even at lesser meetings. The King George V Stakes that year was notable for the defeat of the well-backed favourite Ile De Chypre, who appeared to have the race won but suddenly swerved in the final furlong and unseated jockey Greville Starkey. My theory is that because the stewards had earlier controversially disqualified Royal Gait, subsequent Champion Hurdler, from the Gold Cup in favour of favourite Sadeem, God, or Providence, according to your beliefs, had taken pity on us poor bookmakers and flicked Starkey off Ile De Chypre. An equally unlikely explanation emerged the following year during a drugs trial: one of the defendants claimed he had made a 'stun gun' disguised as a pair of binoculars that emitted an ultrasonic beam which caused the horse to swerve. The implausibility of this claim was compounded by the claim that the horse did not swerve away from the purported sudden intense noise but towards it.

Cheltenham in March 1989 featured many more five-figure bets: £56,000-2,000 each way Maiden Fair in the Supreme; £27,500-20,000 Sabin Du Loir in the Arkle; £50,000-2,500 each way Trapper John in the Sun Alliance Novice Hurdle; £62,500-6,000 Gwho in the NH Chase; £50,000-5,000 each way Rinus in the Ritz Club Handicap Chase. Only Trapper John was placed to give a return, but all those bets were partially hedged, and balanced with winning bets, so the profit on the three days was satisfactory but not colossal.

Royal Ascot that summer generated many such bets: £36,000-16,000 Wadood in the Coventry Stakes (placed second); £24,000-16,000 and £35,000-20,000 Demawend in the Queen's Vase (placed second); £27,500-20,000 Danehill in the Cork & Orrery Stakes (won); £15,000-45,000 Be My Chief in the Chesham Stakes (won); £20,000-45,000 Zero Watt in the Queen Alexandra Stakes (placed third). The end result of the meeting was, however, a substantial loss.

Cheltenham the following March was even busier. Notable bets were £90,000-10,000 Wink Gulliver in the Grand Annual Chase (lost); £90,000-40,000 Champion Hurdle winner Kribensis;

£37,500-30,000 Champion Chase winner Barnbrook Again. Another bad week at the office.

Royal Ascot in 1990 was another roller-coaster ride, with bets of £54,000-12,000 each way Dominion Gold in the Chesham Stakes (placed second), £70,000-21,000 Snowy Owl (placed second) in the Windsor Castle Stakes, £55,000-10,000 Hellenic in the Ribblesdale Stakes (won), £50,000-1,500 each way Cashtal Dazzler in the Britannia Handicap (lost) and £44,000-40,000 Flying Brave (lost) in a race on the Saturday, which was then not part of the Royal Meeting. This time an excellent few days at the office.

Later that summer I felt it was time for another change of car and found that Broughtons of Cheltenham had a new Bentley Turbo for sale. After much negotiation about the allowance for the Mercedes I was part exchanging, we eventually agreed the purchase, and that it would be delivered in August (to gain a later registration) to me at Goodwood. One of Broughtons' directors duly drove the car down to the Millstream Hotel in Bosham where I was staying, and also brought an order form for another new Bentley for a few years later; he was rather taken aback when I declined the invitation to order a replacement, and I kept the new Bentley for more than twenty-five years.

Cheltenham in 1991 brought even more violent changes of fortune. It started with the victory of Destriero in the Supreme Novices Hurdle; I laid £50,000-8,000, and later £25,000-4,000 and another £50,000-8,000 to the same person against it. A bad start, though General Idea, against which I had laid £100,000-20,000, would have been worse. But Remittance Man winning the Arkle put me in front, as I had laid £50,000-20,000 and £75,000-30,000 Uncle Ernie (placed second) and £66,000-1,000 each way outsider General James (lost). Morley Street's Champion Hurdle soon changed that, as I laid £27,000-6,000 and £45,000-10,000 against it; The Iliad would have been even worse, as I had been given £50,000 to put on it, which I hedged at various prices from 8/1 down to 6/1. I also laid £20,000-200 and £40,000-600 each way Rare Holiday, unplaced to my relief. Worse still was

Increasing turnover and a new Bentley

the Stayers Hurdle, where I laid £50,000-20,000 and £55,000-20,000 winner King's Curate. Betting on the Kim Muir was much quieter, and I didn't lay winner Omerta, which brought some relief, but the Grand Annual brought the day to a close with another hefty loss, in spite of laying £100,000-20,000 unplaced Ebony Star. So the day was not only my worst day ever but it was also more than twice the previous record day.

The Sun Alliance Novices Hurdle the next day continued in the same vein with £20,000-8,000 winner Crystal Spirit, though I nearly recovered that loss when Katabatic won the Champion Chase, in which I laid £140,000-40,000 Blitzkreig. £100,000-10,000 each way winner Danny Connors in the Coral Golden Hurdle continued the tale of woe before quiet betting, apart from £40,000-2,000 Mayoran, in the Sun Alliance Chase resulted in a much smaller loss, which almost felt like winning after the previous body-blows. This pattern was repeated in the NH Chase, and when Foyle Fisherman won the Mildmay of Flete Chase unlaid I had a real winning race, though betting was again quiet with no bets with five-figure liabilities. It would have been a record losing day if the day before hadn't already eclipsed the previous record.

The third and last day started with the Triumph Hurdle, which was a much-needed triumph when Oh So Risky came to the rescue, beating Chirkpar into second (£50,000-10,000 each way laid) and unplaced Tomahawk (£100,000-6,000). Lovely Citizen in the Foxhunters was a lovely result in a fairly quiet betting race, and Garrison Savannah was also very welcome in the Gold Cup. In the Ritz Club NH Handicap, in which I laid £30,000-900 Bishops Yarn on the phone to a Devon bookmaker, I felt extremely fortunate not to lay 6/1 third favourite Seagram, the subsequent Grand National winner. I laid £55,000-50,000 Kiichi in the Cathcart, won to my delight by Chatam, before Winnie The Witch won the County Hurdle on which my only payout was on a couple of placed horses. It was as if I had been allowed to write my own results, and I finished the meeting very slightly ahead after expenses!

The Grand National meeting followed a few weeks later. Ever since I started I have found the National a very hard race to win on, whether I was at a point-to-point, another racecourse or Aintree itself, mainly because it is hard to lay enough horses to make a viable book, especially on the rails without a board. So once I had an alternative meeting to go to on National day, usually at Chepstow or Hereford, that was where I would go, even though it would be much quieter.

The first two days of the meeting were busy, with Thursday bringing bets of £40,000-10,000 Smith's Cracker and £40,000-10,000 win, £5,000 place and £52,500-15,000 Danny Connors, both unplaced – a partial recovery from the Danny Connors disaster at Cheltenham. Friday brought bets of £80,000-20,000 Waterloo Boy and £75,000-25,000 in the Melling Chase, where Blazing Walker was a welcome result in spite of £20,000-2,800 being laid. In the Martell Handicap Hurdle, I was not sorry to see Trefelyn Cone finish 1½ lengths ahead of Torwada, against which I had laid £120,000-30,000 – a difference of more than £130,000 between winner and second.

My absence from Aintree the next day caused some surprise, as I was on the rails at Hereford, isolated a long way from the main boards market, where my busiest race was the first with four bets. But I was still able to congratulate myself on the choice of meeting as the first race at Liverpool was won by Blitzkreig at 4/1, and I would definitely have been blitzkrieged if I had been there.

In 1997, after the first two days I went to Aintree early on the Saturday morning to savour the atmosphere and then caught a train to Hereford to catch up with the staff who had gone ahead for the day's racing there. The train passed Chester and Ludlow courses and on the drive home we passed Chepstow and Bath courses, so that by the end of the day I had seen 10% of the country's courses in one day. Meanwhile, the Grand National had been cancelled because of a bomb scare, but it was run two days later instead. I felt that I should support the initiative to stage the race in spite of the attempt to disrupt it, and while many bookmakers who had been there on Saturday did not return, I was probably the only one who missed the Saturday but did attend the Monday. It was a long way to go for just one race, but I was rewarded with a rare winning National when Lord Gyllene won, even though it was among the first few in the betting at 14/1.

On another occasion at Liverpool, the leather bag I used as a moneybag was snatched while I was watching a race. It was smaller than the bag, known as a hod, which board bookmakers used and attached to the rail with a G-clamp. I had noticed a young lad hovering, watching me take cash bets, and I had a feeling he might be up to no good, so every bit of cash went straight into my pocket instead of the bag. I turned my back to watch the race and sure enough when I turned round again after the race, the bag was gone. After the last race I went to the police office to report the theft; they said 'Is this it?' and lo and behold it was! The thief had discarded it, presumably in disgust at finding no money in it, and a man in the crowd had seen what had happened and handed it in. The Question of Sport panel were never asked 'At which racecourse did a rails bookmaker have his bag stolen?' – perhaps it was thought too easy to guess the answer.

The most notable bet on the 1991 Derby was £100,000-20,000 Mystiko; there was also £42,000-6,000 Hector Protector and £45,000-10,000 Corrupt and several smaller bets, so that winner Generous was a good result in spite of a bet of £20,000-2,200. During the next few years there were several bets to win £100,000 or more, mainly at Royal Ascot or the Cheltenham Festival, including a bet of £100,000-120,000 on Tenby, beaten in the 1993 Derby. Laying a large losing bet in a race doesn't necessarily mean it was a winning race; sometimes it just pushed me into laying other horses, including the winner, too much, and sometimes the sum of many lesser, but still substantial, bets outweighed the large losing bet. But on the whole, if the market was strong enough, the system worked.

Chapter 13

Another house move, more large bets and a suspect race

During 1993 I began looking for another house, and after looking at various properties in and around Bath I narrowed the choice down to two live possibilities. One was a terraced house in the Georgian upper town part of Bath, the other a Victorian villa south of the river but near the centre. I eventually settled on the former, as the other one had a magnolia tree growing near the house that I thought might cause problems in the long term. In December I moved in and joined the residents' association, eventually becoming its chairman some years later.

Moving house did not mark any change in the level of business. Further notable bets in the mid-1990s were £200,000-80,000 Oh So Risky, second to Flakey Dove in the 1994 Champion Hurdle; £100,000-20,000 Miracle Man, which looked beaten in a handicap hurdle at Cheltenham in 1995 but got up to win by a short head from skinner Pragada – a difference of more than £127,000 to turn a good winning day into a losing one; £200,000-100,000 Treble Bob, whose SP was 9/4, demonstrating the strength of the Cheltenham market at that time – it came a close third in the Sun Alliance Novice Hurdle. The 1996 Grand National featured a bet of £200,000-12,000 each way Wylde Hide, unplaced. In the Wokingham Stakes at Royal Ascot in 1996 I laid 100,000-10,000 each way Prince Babar and £100,000-14,000 each way Green Perfume. They were close up second and fourth respectively to 33/1 shot Emerging Market, which I hadn't laid, but I still lost £27,727 on the race, which I claim as a record for the largest amount a bookmaker has lost on a race without laying the winner.

Another race I recall, this time with a sour taste, was the race won at Chepstow by Jibbereen on 10 October 1995. It was a challenge race for six flat jockeys against six jump jockeys over seven furlongs, and it was staged (a word used advisedly) to mark the comeback of jockey Declan Murphy from a nasty head injury. The conditions stipulated that the twelve jockeys would be chosen by Chepstow racecourse and allocated to the runners by random ballot the day before the race. I laid only one bet on the horse – £30,000-6,000 – and though I have had any number of worse losing races, never have I had such a strong feeling of being stitched up. The horse started at 3/1 and was in front from the start; it transpired that Declan Murphy had been riding it out days before the 'random' ballot.

I and others complained to the Jockey Club and suggested that because of the pattern of the ballot for riders, the pattern of the betting and the pattern of the race, there was a lot to investigate and there was a lot of comment and correspondence in the press and elsewhere along the same lines. I am by no means suggesting that this was an instance of a race with only one trier, but it was notable that the loudest protesters about calls for an inquiry were the trainer and jockey of the winner, yet if any race is to be fixed, it is not the intended winner who has to be involved in the plot as he just has to be allowed to do his best – it is the other runners who have to be 'got at'. It reminded me of the line from Hamlet: 'the lady doth protest too much methinks'.

In the end, whatever half-hearted inquiry there was resulted in a whitewash of all concerned, to the disappointment of myself and many others. At the end of the year, nominations were invited in the racing press for ride of the year. I wrote in to nominate Declan Murphy's ride on Jibereen, commending his skill in securing the ride on the favourite, his foresight in riding out the very horse he would be balloted to ride days later, and his deft criticism of anyone daring to question anything about the race or circumstances surrounding it, thus ensuring that more column inches were devoted to his ride than any other that year. My nomination was ignored.

Another memorable day was Frankie Dettori's so-called Magnificent Seven when he rode all seven winners at Ascot on 25 September 1996, though I prefer to call it the Malevolent Seven – nothing magnificent about it for me or other bookmakers at Ascot that day. The phone was never so busy that day once Frankie had won the fourth race on Decorated Hero, which was a winner for me aided by £50,000-20,000 each way High Summer being unplaced. Then things turned nasty. More than £40,000 came from off-course bookmakers for the fifth winner, the ominously named Fatefully; much of it was hedged and £100,000-8,000 each way Ninja, unplaced, helped to soften the blow. In the next race, well over £50,000 came for winner Lochangel, an unwelcome result in spite of much hedging.

Frankie's last mount was Fujiyama Crest, which had been 10/1 or bigger before racing, and now off-course bookmakers were scrambling to get on at almost any price. The betting got under way with £100,000-14,000 and £100,000-16,000 each way Durham before an avalanche of phone bets arrived from bookmakers all over the country for Fujiyama Crest, totalling £242,500. I, and the bookmakers I was hedging with, thought we were being clever laying at 9/4 and 2/1 a horse whose chance had earlier been rated 10/1. The activity was so hectic that it was impossible to know what the liability was, but I did know that I didn't want the horse to win. But it did, and to make things worse, I had laid £100,000-8,000 each way Ivor's Flutter, which finished fourth.

Every weekend, sending cheques out on Sunday before the losing accounts were settled resulted in adverse cash flow, but that week was exceptional, especially as even the hedging proceeds were not forthcoming as quickly as they should have been – in fact I still haven't collected them all. One off-course bookmaker later told me that when he read about the carnage in the Ascot ring and elsewhere that Frankie had caused, he was rather nervous about collecting, and was relieved to receive his cheque with the usual promptness. However, I was obliged to delay settlement to my largest creditor, the Tote, and I am grateful for their forbearance. I believe they knew I would pay given time, and I always knew I would pay them, and I did indeed pay in 'easy' instalments in due course.

There were fewer six-figure bets at Cheltenham in 1997 than in the preceding years, but Epsom and Ascot reverted to type. I made a slight loss on the Oaks in spite of £100,000-11,000 each way Ebadiyla, unplaced, but the Derby was better with £100,000-125,000 losing favourite Entrepreneur, and 1998 brought a similar story.

The biggest bet I ever laid on coursing was £30,000-1,000 against Tintern Abbey in the 2003 Waterloo Cup. To my surprise he kept getting through the early rounds, but I kept thinking, well he's still in, but he can't win. But come the final day, he was still there in the semi-final! Whenever I went to Hereford racecourse there was a choice of two routes, either via the M5 or up the Wye Valley, passing the ruins of Tintern Abbey; I said if this dog wins, I'll never want to go to Hereford that way again. Fortunately, he was knocked out of the Cup in his semi-final.

A feature of the 1990s was the increased publicity I was receiving as a result of my turnover, which peaked at £21 million one year. This was in the form of both full-page articles and minor snippets, mainly in the Racing Post and now defunct Sporting Life, but also in many other papers and magazines, including The Times, Sunday Times, Guardian, Observer Magazine, Independent, Daily Express, Sunday Express, Mail On Sunday, The Sun, London Evening Standard, Western Daily Press, Bath & West Chronicle, and even the Irish Sunday Tribune and Dublin Evening Herald. In the run-up to Cheltenham in 1993, I was described in the Standard as 'fabulously wealthy', which just shows that you can't believe everything you read in the newspapers. What you can believe is that I am probably the only bookmaker to have had a nine-page write-up in a stud book, when I was awarded the Jack Chadwick Trophy for 'services to coursing' in 2004, as reported in the Greyhound Stud Book.

Paul Haigh in the Racing Post once described me as 'bookmaker to the stars', a reference to the leading owners and trainers, such as Barney Curley, J.P. McManus and Michael Tabor, and other racing establishment figures who were clients. Other clients included professional punters, such as Harry Findlay, a very quiet man except when he was awake, businessmen such as prolific owner and punter Geoffrey Greenwood, who is credited with inventing the open-plan office, titled individuals and well-known figures from the sporting, pop music and entertainment worlds. At the time of the House of Lords reform, I asked Lord Ailesbury if he was one of the peers who had got the sack from the Lords, to which he replied, 'Yes, and from the Tote'; he seemed to be more upset about losing his Tote account than his seat in the Lords!

Professional punter Patrick Veitch, in his book Enemy Number One, wrote that he had £12,000 at 15/8 on the winner of the third race at Bath in May 1996 and that he saw me leaving the course, supposedly disgruntled, straight afterwards. In fact his bet was £10,000 at 7/4, but it certainly wasn't me that he saw leaving. The only reason I would leave any meeting early would be to go to another meeting, the sole exception being in the early days of bumpers (NH flat races) in England when they were so uncompetitive that they were virtually schooling races and I would leave before they were run to avoid getting stitched up. I wish I had left after the third race at Bath that day, as in the next race I laid £60,000-20,000 each way the winner and £60,000-5,000 each way the second; in the fifth race I laid £50,000-50,000 the winner and £45,000-15,000 each way the last winner. Patrick also mentioned that he had heard that Michael Tabor had had a large winning bet at Ascot earlier that month, on a day when he wasn't there, which illustrates how incorrect rumours get around. One year I heard a rumour that, at Cheltenham, I had won a large amount that was more than I had even taken, but it's nice to have my credit rating sent through the roof in this way.

At one point in the 1990s the BHA announced that there was to be major revision of race-planning, which would result in larger fields, more competitive racing and less odds-on runners. This was presented as marvellous news for bookmakers, which it probably was for most, especially the large multiples, but I received this news with dismay. I always preferred to have some short-priced favourites to get stuck into, and the races I disliked most were the big wide open handicaps, the nadir being the 1996 Wokingham mentioned in the previous chapter. I didn't want to read or hear that the day's card was going to be really hard for punters and a bookies' bonanza; I wanted to hear people saying 'We're going to send those ghastly bookies home skint today'!

I always aimed to lay as many different horses as I could, but without a board to advertise all prices at once, it was usually possible to lay only four or five properly, if that, and I would rather lay five horses out of seven or eight than five out of twenty. Now that rails bookmakers have boards, they have a better prospect of laying a good proportion of the whole field in any race. But what was just as important was having a feel for the market on any particular day, so that when I took a sizable bet I could gauge how likely I was to bet up to it on the other runners and how much I should hedge, and that remains the case today. Needless to say, I didn't always get it right.

Another, less welcome, feature of the 1990s was the dialogue between the NAB and the RCA[1] about updating the administration and other aspects of the betting ring, including the rails. By the beginning of 1998, the long-running talks about major reforms to racecourse betting were coming to a head, and I was beginning to realise that my days as an independent racecourse bookmaker were numbered, as related in the following chapter.

---

1. NAB: National Association of Bookmakers. RCA: Racecourse Association.

Chapter 14

Bookmaking politics and the threat to the betting ring

I had joined the local bookmakers' association, the West of England Bookmakers' Association, in October 1971, not long after moving to Devizes. A few years later, my first venture into bookmaker politics was not propitious. There were vacancies on its council, so along with a few other candidates I put myself forward to be elected and tied for the last position. President Ron Harrison was an office bookmaker in Weston-super-Mare and did not know much about me, so his casting vote went to the other runner, of whom it is fair to say that he was not the best example of our profession. In April 1975 I did become a council member, and encouraged and supported by Eddie Baxter (of Avalon Turf) went on to become the Association's representative at Pitch Rules meetings in London of the National Association of Bookmakers to which it was affiliated, and later still to become the WoEBA's president, thus becoming in 1986 the Association's representative on the NAB board, which met in London four or five times a year.

The NAB then consisted of twelve member associations of varying sizes, including one from Wales and three from Scotland. The largest were the Northern and Southern associations, with the West of England being one of the smaller ones; most racecourse bookmakers were members of one of the affiliated associations, as were most off-course bookmakers until the formation of the Betting Office Licensees Association in 1973. It was represented on the Levy

Board, and administered pitches in all rings at all racecourses, with the exception of the Hill at Epsom. It also dealt with other matters concerning both on- and off-course bookmakers.

The Fergusson scheme, by which order was brought to pitch administration to replace the chaos that had ruled previously, began in 1958. Each association elected a pitch committee from its members to administer the allocation and use of pitches in its own area in accordance with the National Pitch Rules drawn up by the NAB, in conjunction with the RCA, and individual racecourses were relieved of any need to get involved with pitch matters on their own courses. The scheme was funded by a surcharge on bookmakers' daily attendances to operate; pitch committee members gave their time voluntarily, but the fund met office expenses, travel expenses to local and national meetings concerning pitch matters, and other necessary expenses. There were regular national meetings to keep rules up to date as new circumstances arose, and to hear appeals against decisions made by pitch committees.

In the early days of the scheme, there were few if any waiting lists, and each course had at least two or three rings, but as time went on, rings closed or were combined, and waiting lists grew and grew, which as stated earlier was why I had to go on the rails to continue my career. For instance, I applied for a Tatts pitch at Towcester when I got my licence in 1971 and still hadn't reached the top of it by 1998. Older pitch holders would hang on well past retirement age because, unlike in most businesses, those who had built up a business over many years could not sell out for a lump sum, and pitches could be passed on only to their children who had worked regularly with them. Others who lacked either the wherewithal or inclination to be bookmakers became landlords instead, finding a wannabe bookmaker to finance them, thus queue-jumping the waiting lists.

Towards the end of the 1980s, the stagnation in the ring had been recognised as a major problem, and alternatives were sought to the 'dead men's shoes' system that had prevailed over the last decades.

Many schemes were proposed and examined, and information about how pitches were traded in Ireland, Australia and South Africa was obtained. There was a consensus that some form of buying and selling pitches was needed; after much discussion, a scheme was hammered out, but when advice was sought on the tax implications, which were manifold, it was put in abeyance.

The RCA was also becoming concerned that the betting ring had not moved with the times, and also that they were not getting enough money from bookmakers. They failed to realise that the annual financial contribution from on-course bookmakers' daily payments of around £3 million was only a small part of their worth to racecourses, as without the attraction of the betting ring attendances would be comparable to those at French racecourses, where the tote monopoly leaves them devoid of the atmosphere and excitement generated by the existence of a lively betting market. However, so as to increase their income without sacrificing the limit of five times admission fees enshrined in law for the protection of the betting public, the NAB agreed a scheme to allow more waiting-list bookmakers to operate when there was room. With a display of disingenuousness that would be repeated several times over the next few years of talks, the RCA attempted to expand the scheme beyond what had been agreed.

The RCA also felt that the betting facilities available to their customers in the most expensive area, the Members' Enclosure, now generally termed the Premier Enclosure, were inadequate, and that they should be improved. The nature of this formerly exclusive enclosure had indeed changed over the years: when I joined Cheltenham as a junior annual member in the late 1960s, not only did I have to find two nominators who were already members but they also had to write letters of recommendation to confirm that I was suitable. Talks between the RCA and NAB began in 1991 with the RCA insisting that the emphasis was not on increasing revenue for courses but improving the experience for their customers. We were proved right not to believe them when they later proposed a

3% levy on turnover, which would have undone all the good work in persuading the government to remove the 4% turnover tax and possibly led to its re-imposition.

I had joined the Rails Bookmakers Association (RBA) in 1987 and was one of few of its members who in 1991 did not support its aim to lobby for boards on the rails, as I thought that it would necessitate a complete reallocation of all pitches under the rule governing alterations to enclosures if the worst pitches were suddenly turned into the best pitches. The RBA proceeded to write to the RCA claiming that the Office of Fair Trading was likely to view the rule forbidding display of prices as a restraint of trade. I continued to state in NAB board meetings that boards on rails should not happen without a complete reallocation.

Meanwhile, Chepstow racecourse decided they didn't want to abide by the Pitch Rules, which, as a member of the RCA, they had committed to, and barred some bookmakers from operating. The NAB felt that Chepstow had no right to ignore the Rules, and the row rumbled on until when in February 1992, because the principle of the Fergusson scheme being binding on all courses was so important, the NAB sought an injunction to bring Chepstow to heel. I was a joint plaintiff with the NAB in the case in the High Court, which was successful. Coincidentally, I later sold my house to the judge who had heard the case, though it's unlikely that he realised the connection.

The court judgement was that the Fergusson scheme, and the consequent Pitch Rules, were binding on all racecourses, but it was also ruled that the RCA had the right to terminate the scheme on twelve months' notice, whereas the original scheme did not have any mechanism for termination. No system of buying and selling pitches would work if there was no security of tenure, so it was back to the drawing board. Talks resumed with the aim of achieving better provision of betting facilities and a method of transferring pitches, provided security of tenure could be assured; I was heavily involved in this process, including appearing with Sir Paul Fox on the weekly Saturday Morning Line programme in 1994.

In 1992, long-standing NAB chairman Alfie Bruce resigned from the post, and in March 1993 an election was held for a new chairman. I put myself forward, with the approval of the West of England Association, along with Peter Watson of the Northern Association and Norman Miller of the Scottish Association. I believe Peter was far more anxious to win the race than either Norman or myself, and he was generally regarded as favourite. I recall that when Alan Delmonte, now chief executive of the Levy Board but then a Sporting Life journalist, rang me and asked whether I was confident of winning the ballot, I replied that I was confident only of getting my own vote. Peter duly romped home, and I was narrowly elected as treasurer. I considered Peter eminently suitable for the chairmanship and we served together on many of the forthcoming negotiations with the RCA's team. In 1995 I was elected as Vice-chairman, though I declined to accept the modest stipend attached to the position on principle, as I was there to serve the profession, not for personal gain.

The NAB/RCA talks rumbled on, and more than once we thought that agreement had been reached only for the RCA to backtrack. During this time two things became clear: that the RCA could not be relied on to ensure that all racecourses kept to any agreement made, and that they saw boards on rails as an essential element of modernising betting facilities in the top enclosures. As the RCA held the Sword of Damocles in the form of the right to give notice of termination of the Fergusson scheme, they had the upper hand on this issue, so the best policy was not to refuse to countenance it but to find a way that would be fair to all pitch holders involved.

I spent many hours over the next few years attempting to devise schemes that would allow at least some boards on rails, would be fair to all bookmakers, would create movement, raise some return for racecourses (which would be necessary for the RCA to accept it) – and be workable. But too many of the NAB directors, guided by the members of the associations they represented, wanted to dig their heels in and oppose any agreement that would permit boards on rails. The Welsh Association's director, Mel Jones (once described to me as 'a man of limited intellect', which I thought – at the time – a bit harsh), said the NAB should oppose any suggestion of boards on rails 'right up to the wire'. I wanted to point out that the wire he wanted to get so close to had 30,000 volts running through it.

In October 1997 the RCA understandably lost patience with the collective intransigence of the NAB board and gave twelve months' notice that the Fergusson scheme would terminate. The Levy Board, having realised that this was probably imminent, took legal advice about their powers in relation to regulation of betting areas and concluded that, in the event of termination of the Fergusson scheme, they should step in. The Levy Board accordingly set up a Review Committee comprising three independent Levy Board members, chaired by Sir John Sparrow, to make arrangements for future pitch administration; three meetings were held to hear evidence in February 1998, where the RCA, NAB and RBA were all represented and I was part of the NAB delegation. That Committee reported to the Levy Board in March, with a recommendation that a National Joint Pitch Council (NJPC) be formed to take over pitch administration the following October when the twelve months' notice period expired.

Chapter 15

They know not what they do

The timeframe for the formation of the NJPC to set up a new pitch administration system was very tight considering what had to be done. First, the members of the Council itself had to be found, then they had to recruit staff, determine policies on several matters, guided by the Levy Board's Review, draw up a completely new rule book in spite of having no experience of the subject, and set a budget on the basis of projections that would necessarily be based on guesswork.

An early indication of their incompetence came in May 1998 with the first draft of pitch rules, which contained this gem:

> *12.11 No Authorised Bookmaker shall negotiate or receive bets on any horserace other than "in Running".*

In other words, we would have to wait for a race to start before we could take any bets on it! Several subsequent drafts were issued, but each one prompted much detailed correspondence from me pointing out the flaws in particular rules, including explaining why they were flawed, and that a system which was intended to enhance service to customers was going to reduce the service I could give.

The concerns I had about the rules being drafted are too numerous to list, but one of my main ones was the attendance rule, which stipulated that a bookmaker had to attend a third of the meetings at each course where he had a pitch, and that missing three successive meetings would result in the loss of his pitch. The NAB rulebook had also had rules to discourage non-attendance, which were necessary to ensure there were enough bookmakers to form a reasonable betting market, but the difference was that while the NAB accepted attendance at another race meeting as an acceptable excuse, the NJPC rules would not. When I looked at my planned attendances for the fixture list for 1998 I found that in attending 246 days at 24 different courses, I would attend less than a third of fixtures at seven of those courses, and possibly three more, as that calculation made no allowance for holidays, cancellations or extra fixtures. I wanted to remain a full-time bookmaker, and my staff wanted to be full-time staff.

I didn't dispute the need for a reasonable number of bookmakers at even the quietest meetings, but it should have been obvious that, with waiting lists numbered in the hundreds and the dam about to burst to let them in when auctions of pitches started, there would be no shortage of bookmakers willing and eager to fill the rings. But what was proposed was like imposing a hosepipe ban in the Ruhr Valley after the Dambusters had bombed the Möhne Dam. I pointed out that if bookmakers were being forced to give up some of their courses, the stronger bookmakers would tend to keep their pitches only at larger courses, leaving smaller courses with weakened markets even on days when they were the principal meeting. This was ignored, and it emerged that the NJPC wanted to force sales to enable them to fund the salaries of those who would be doing what bookmaker members of associations had long been doing for nothing.

Another major concern was that the designated numbers of bookmakers allowed to operate on each day would render the business unviable on ordinary days. It seemed that betting rings would include not just too many bookmakers, but too many amateur bookmakers. In any business it is hard to compete with rivals who either don't need to make it pay or don't know how to make it pay. And in no other field of commerce are there so many businesses in a confined space all trying to sell the same thing.

Many of the other rules that I complained about were less significant, though still irritating if taken separately, but as a whole they added up to a regime that I was not looking forward to operating under. It had become apparent that not only did they not know what they were doing but also that they didn't even realise that they didn't know what they were doing.

An added complication was that I was no longer in a position to expound my views on the new system in any official capacity to the NJPC, but had to do so as an individual. In April I was voted out of office as president of the West of England Association and therefore automatically was no longer a director of the NAB. I think the main reasons were because I remained a member of the RBA, even though I always supported NAB policy at their meetings, and that I had been perceived as not being hawkish enough in opposing the RCA in the negotiations, including on the boards on rails issue, although it had been the stubbornness of other NAB directors that had led to the current situation. I was also criticised because, in the election for a new NAB chairman, I wanted to support Norman Miller, while others favoured David Boden, who I had to vote for reluctantly as mandated and who did become the new chairman. This was disappointing after working hard to represent the interests of members, without regard to my own interests, by accepting the reality of what could and could not be achieved. I believe I was proved right on both counts, but the old saying that 'politics is the art of the possible' had been ignored.

Shortly afterwards I was expelled from the RBA for not supporting their aim of boards on rails for current rails pitch holders without any reallocation. I said at the time that expelling any member who doesn't agree with the majority doesn't reflect well on any association; this comment was printed by the Racing Post among a group of quotes by racing individuals, presumably because the Post thought it was fair comment.

Under David Boden, the NAB launched a judicial review to test whether the Levy Board was entitled to impose the NJPC. This failed, but even if it had been ruled that the Board was acting ultra vires, the RCA would still have taken over the formation of the NJPC, so it was an expensive and futile move. The NAB had already been advised by a QC that fighting the Board in court would 'end in tears'; this proved correct, and he could have added 'much wailing and gnashing of teeth'. My view was that David's only talent was as a Mr Bean impersonator; after overseeing a near mortal blow to the NAB, he soon departed the bookmaking business.

The nascent NJPC carried on with the tasks of drawing up seniority lists for all rings on all racecourses and designating numbers of bookmakers for each race day, complicated processes that were necessarily rushed. This resulted in many appeals from bookmakers, including me, querying the seniority ascribed to them; because of the time constraints, some appeals were not given the thorough hearing they deserved.

The voluminous correspondence I had sent to the NJPC on many aspects of the rules had not had much impact, and the new arrangements duly came into operation in early October. We had been promised many things in this brave new world for betting rings: efficient administration, mains electricity for computers and suchlike at every pitch position, screens in the ring showing away races and other information to keep punters in the ring, and the opportunity for bookmakers in Members' enclosures. The first broken promise was electricity at every pitch, and bookmakers would be allowed in Members only if they agreed to pay 5% of their turnover. Screens in the ring never materialised; the large screens now in place at most meetings partly compensate, though they do not show many away races, or even a static display of the last home race result, as used to be shown on the old number boards. And efficient administration, as far as viability was concerned, was always a long odds against shot in my view.

Would-be bookmakers were urged to buy pitches that they could later leave to their grandchildren. As before, what bookmakers would own was not real estate, with air space and mineral rights, but the right to bet in a specified relative position, more accurately described as a pick number rather than a pitch. But whereas this right was portrayed as freehold, the RCA later announced that that arrangement would cease at a given date in the future, and that in effect the freehold was altered to leasehold. The present-day stands, or joints, that pitch holders would be required to use instead of the tripod type are far less portable; once when I travelled by train to occupy my Tatts pitch at Yarmouth, I cycled 10 miles with my old-style joint on the back from Devizes to Pewsey station, but when I picked up a new joint for Colin Webster at Sandown one day, it wouldn't all fit in the boot of the Bentley.

With the new regime in place, would the ring be revitalised and strengthened, and attract increased attendances? Or had the baby been thrown out with the bathwater?

Chapter 16

Notice to quit and joining Corals

It wasn't long before I was starting to ask myself whether I wanted to carry on. I had always thought that I would remain on the rails almost for ever, like Hector McDonald who was still betting on the rails well into his 80s, but I was still well under normal retirement age. Just as in my school days the realisation that my vocation was bookmaking was gradual, so now the thought that it was time to get out was also creeping up on me – not a decision to be taken lightly, as it had only ever been what I wanted to do. When an article appeared in the Racing Post in late November saying I was thinking of quitting, many people didn't think I meant it and was bluffing to provoke some action from the NJPC – but I did mean it and I wrote to Levy Board chief executive Rodney Brack to say so.

By December my disillusionment was complete. There were going to be too many amateur bookmakers to compete with, the expenses were going to rocket, the business was going to be regulated by people who had little understanding of bookmaking or pitch administration, and I was not going either to make it pay or to enjoy working on course as I had done so far. Another factor in the back of my mind was that I was beginning to wonder whether the policing of racing's integrity was as rigorous as it should be. I had always said that the fact that I could bet to all comers, never closing a winning account and laying any horses that punters wanted to back, and not get wiped out, was a good indication that British racing was straight, but after the Jibereen incident and its aftermath, or rather lack of aftermath, I was starting to say it with less conviction.

In November I fulfilled a long-held ambition to visit Australia, travelling round by train, visiting a friend and some distant relatives in Sydney, and taking in the Melbourne Cup and a few other race meetings. When I returned to England, I heard there had been a rumour that I had gone there on a reconnaissance mission with a view to setting up in business down under. In fact, the thought hadn't even occurred to me, and if it had, my visit to Randwick, the main racecourse in New South Wales, would have put me off. I arrived there a little late, rushed in and looked at the group of bookmakers behind the grandstand, and went up into the stand to watch the race. It was deserted, and I thought there had been a bomb scare! Flemington racecourse at Melbourne was of course much busier, but much as I enjoyed my time in Australia, uprooting myself to move there was never an option.

My plan was to try to sell my rails pitches as one lot, hoping to sell myself with them, and auction my boards pitches individually. The first auction was at Sandown, where I entered nos. 29 at Ludlow and 45 at Southwell without reserve; Ludlow fetched £3,000, but there was no bid for Southwell – I said it was the only pitch in the auction that had fetched its true value – and it took several auctions before it was sold for the minimum bid of £250.

I put the other boards pitches in forthcoming auctions, again without reserves, while I sought a buyer for all my rails pitches. In another daft move by the NJPC, they decreed that when a pitch was sold, the vendor's attendance record went with it, so that it was necessary for any retiring bookmaker to keep attending or risk rendering his pitches unsaleable. So I had to keep going to those courses reluctantly, possibly displacing another bookmaker lower down the list who actually wanted to operate. In January 1999, a photo appeared on the front page of the Racing Post showing me offering evens each of fourteen runners in a race at Wincanton the previous day; on the next page, journalist Matt Chapman quoted my explanation that I had been forced to come to keep the pitch.

Notice to quit and joining Corals

Matt also quoted NJPC chairman Richard Marriott as saying that the NJPC cannot interfere with bookmakers' terms of trade or make someone put up sensible prices. Nevertheless a few days later I received from Mr Marriott a written warning that I was guilty of breaking two pitch rules by offering false prices and distorting the betting market and SP. I replied, with a copy to the Racing Post, pointing out that he had misunderstood the purpose of the relevant rule, which had been copied from the NAB rules, and which was to stop once-common 'SP jobs' where bookmakers would offer over the odds purely to create an inflated SP. I also said that SP returners have always ignored prices under the odds for horses that a bookmaker did not wish to lay, that my actions would have had no effect on SP, and that it was the NJPC who were adversely affecting the integrity of SP, by forcing reluctant bookmakers to operate and allowing too many bookmakers. It was yet another example of the fundamental lack of understanding of racecourse bookmaking by the NJPC.

I thought that there were two runners for the purchase of my rails pitches: the Tote, which had held racecourse pitches in the 1970s, and Corals. The Tote did show some interest initially, but in the end it was Corals and the sale was announced in March at Sandown on the Friday before Cheltenham, with my first day betting under the Coral banner at Sandown the following day. I also persuaded the firm to take on my longstanding clerk, John Durston, as he was fast, accurate, honest and discreet, even if not the most convivial travelling companion, and it was agreed that I could continue to bet at the Waterloo Cup in my own name.

I knew that switching from being self-employed as a one-man business to being a corporate representative would be a bit of a culture shock. When bookmakers, or rather licence-holders cum pitch landlords who have always been financed, suddenly have to bet with their own money they usually struggle, but I was moving in the opposite direction. I was once told that I might find the change harder than expected, but I was not too concerned. I was being hired for my experience and proven ability to make it pay, and Coral spokesman Simon Clare was quoted in the press as saying that I would not be restricted in any way. Corals bought more rails pitches at some of the courses where I hadn't bet, such as Newmarket, Chester and Doncaster, and I was sent up to the pitch auction at Perth to buy a pitch at Ayr. I took these purchases as a vote of confidence in the future of our racecourse operation, and I was looking forward to betting with an additional large group of existing Coral clients, without the burden of sending out accounts each weekend, and to betting at courses I had not previously operated at.

The reality soon turned out differently. Many of my clients were sent letters closing their accounts; many punters regard such missives as a nuisance but also a compliment, but like German Iron Cross medals handed out in the First World War, or minor university degrees in modern Britain, they became so numerous as to be devalued. Everyone else who survived this pogrom was still treated with great caution as a potential winner. There was one punter I recall of whom the office was so worried about whether he might win that they forgot to worry about whether he might fail to pay, and sure enough he lost and knocked. I had never closed any account for winning, as I took the view that it wasn't necessary to beat every single punter. I hadn't even kept records of whether any individuals won or lost over time; I had always wanted to lay as many horses in each race as possible, and not deny anyone the chance to take a price I was offering.

I knew that I would be informed of horses that had been well backed in the office and in the firm's shops, and that I would have to take that into account, but the amount of interference from the office went way beyond that. I was often told of horses that I should be careful with because they were well fancied, and it was a standing joke with my clerk how bad these 'tips' were. In a five-horse race at Chester once, I was told that one horse had been well backed, and there were two others to be wary of. I said to John that we should be having a reversed forecast on the remaining two runners, but unfortunately we failed to act on that winning strategy. Sometimes when I laid a bet on the course, the office would tell the other staff, without first telling me, to hedge it all in the ring; so when we had a winning day, the office people were geniuses, but on a losing day, I was a clueless idiot. Part of the deal had been that I would receive a percentage of any profits, but I wasn't being given the chance to make any.

Chapter 17

Redundancy and retirement to stud

Two major family events occurred during my time with Corals. A few years earlier my cousin Peter had disappeared in France where he was living and working and had been found dead weeks later in the River Oise, victim of an apparent robbery and attack. The culprit was eventually charged and tried in Beauvais, and I, along with Peter's sister, mother and my mother, went to the trial. My French wasn't good enough to follow everything, but I understood the gist of the proceedings, and I was pleased to be present to support my aunt. The culmination was a guilty verdict and a sentence of twenty years.

The second event was my marriage in 2001 to Michelle. We had met by chance a few years earlier when I had gone to London for the Countryside Rally in Hyde Park. In the evening I went to a backgammon club off Brompton Road and played in a minor tournament in which I was beaten in the semi-final; I dashed out to hail a taxi to Paddington Station hoping to catch the last train to Bath at 11.30. The taxi driver did his best for what was always a long shot, but though I just missed the 11.30, there was a train to South Wales, stopping at Bristol Parkway, at 11.40, so I caught that and on arrival at Bristol Parkway got into a taxi for Bath.

Before the taxi drove off, a railwayman came up to say that there was another passenger for Bath if I didn't mind sharing, so off we went to Bath. She had also gone to London for the day to the British Museum where she had previously worked as a curator. During the journey I learned that she was now the curator of the Museum of East

Asian Art in Bath, which I had never felt the need to visit even though it was only a couple of furlongs from my home, but I went there a few days later and things developed from then. For us to meet, we both had to arrive at Paddington in that ten-minute window between 11.30 and 11.40; and if I had won the backgammon semi-final, I would have stayed for the final and missed both trains. I thought I was winning in the last game of the match until my opponent threw a double six; I believe it is the most expensive defeat in the 3,000-year history of backgammon! We had a gathering at a Bath race meeting the evening before the ceremony, which many thought would not occur until both the Pope and the Dalai Lama had got hitched.

It was not long after the wedding that Corals decided to reduce their course operation and made me redundant, which did not upset me unduly; perhaps I just wasn't suited to corporate life. When I sold my pitches to Corals, I had suggested that there should be a contingency that if boards on rails became a reality, I should receive an extra percentage of the sale price, but it was argued that I would benefit anyway as it would enable me to share in greater profits. Disappointing as it was that the undertaking to let me bet in my own way was broken so soon, I was not enjoying it and I was content to retire to stud and breed two sons, Charles and Thomas. However, I was left wondering whether it had been their plan all along, to dump me and reap the full benefit of boards on rails when they sold all the pitches for much more than they had bought them for, and whether they had acted in bad faith from the start.

Meanwhile, I continued to go racing, averaging two or three days a week. At that time, the Internet was developing rapidly and betting exchanges were being launched, initially with little liquidity until Betfair and main rivals Flutter were amalgamated. This new concept in betting was seen by most bookmakers as the enemy, but I met up with Paul Williams, who had the idea of forming a consortium of bookmakers to create their own betting exchange, and I agreed to join forces with him to recruit as many bookmakers as we could, and to build our own exchange.

The advent of betting exchanges was the equivalent of the coming of supermarkets in the grocery trade. Originally you would go up to the counter and tell the shop assistant the various food stuffs you wanted, and he or she would fetch the items from the shelves before totting up the cost. Then someone realised that it would be more efficient, and allow a greater range of products, if the customer were to select what they wanted from the displays and bring it all to the till; thus the supermarket was born. In those early competitive days of supermarkets, cartoonist David Langdon produced a drawing of two tic-tac men signalling prices of goods between shops!

In the same way, the exchange concept, instead of balancing bets on different horses in each race, switched to balancing back and lay bets on each horse separately, and also introduced the self-service element by allowing punters to invite back or lay bets at their own stated odds. One common criticism of the exchange model is that it can facilitate profiting from inside information or non-triers, but I liken it to lighting in a car park: the lights might make it easier for a thief to see what he's doing, but it also makes it easier to catch him, and many nefarious betting coups have been rumbled by the information of betting patterns on exchanges. And who wouldn't prefer to park in a well-lit car park with CCTV rather than down a dark side street?

Some bookmakers were reluctant to get involved because they felt it was like turkeys voting for Christmas, to which we responded that Christmas was coming anyway, so all the more reason to join in – if you can't beat 'em, join 'em. We travelled all over the country, and to Ireland, to talk to both on- and off-course bookmakers to persuade them that it would be another string to their bow when they were operating, and we also went to Toronto one cold December to help with the writing of the software.

Eventually we got the exchange, which we named Betmart, up and running, and by a remarkable coincidence had an office in not only the same county, not only in the same city, but in the same road where I had lived in Nottingham in my early years. Concentrating mainly on horseracing and English and Scottish League football, we worked hard on building up the liquidity and at one point were ahead of Betdaq in what we offered on horseracing in terms of odds and liquidity. However, we failed to recruit enough bookmakers to progress, and we were undercapitalised, making effective advertising difficult, so although we got to the end of the runway, we couldn't take off – which was better than taking off and crashing, as rival exchange Sporting Options did. Paul and I remained friends and often went racing together until some years later he contracted cancer and died – a sad loss.

In February 2005, just before the new law banning hunting and coursing came into effect, the last Waterloo Cup was held. The first occasion my name had seen the light of day on a bookmaking joint was at the Waterloo Cup of 1971, and now the last time was also to be at the same meeting. My wife and 1-year-old first son accompanied me and I surprised myself by not shedding a tear for the end of several decades of enjoyment of the sport. Continued attendance at the National Coursing Festival in Clonmel and the Irish Cup near Limerick offered some respite, but I still miss being involved in the British version.

Not long afterwards, the Gambling Commission came into being, with consequent radical changes to the licensing regime. To renew my licence for three years had cost £20, and it came in the form of one side of A4 paper; under the Commission, it would cost several hundred a year, with lots of intrusive questions, and comprise more than thirty pages of red tape. Thirty-plus years of building a reputation would have counted for nothing in their assessment of my suitability, in contrast to when betting shops were legalised, and any conviction for illegal betting in the area was an advantage in applying for a betting shop licence. Under the old system, I would have kept the licence in force, but with no desire to come back into a business so different to what I had known, I felt no inclination to do so.

Heathorns, founded by Alec Heathorn in 1890, one of the oldest established bookmakers (1890) still extant, was one of the firms associated with my first employer, Beresford & Smith. It was now owned by an international firm based in Malta, and an opportunity arose to join them to represent them on course. I had left my first job there in 1966 because I didn't look like getting on the course with them, but I always knew that if I waited long enough, they would want me back! Perhaps we started with a bad omen when we turned up to the wrong court in London to apply for the licence and had to make a mad dash to the correct court. In 2006 at the first Royal Ascot after the new stand was built, our turnover on the entire thirty races, even with a board displaying odds, was less than I used to average per race there on my own without a board, and we made little progress after that on the half-dozen pitches the firm had before calling a halt to the venture. The owner of the business, Thomas Taulé, once asked me to sign minutes of a directors' meeting that I hadn't attended, which I refused to do. The pitches were sold, but shortly afterwards I was back on the rails representing Jennings, a long-established family firm in Essex. They were easier to work with as they were steeped in the business, but there weren't enough pitches to build a clientele for a sustainable business, so my presence on the rails came to an end.

Chapter 18

Looking back

'Of making many books there is no end', according to Ecclesiastes 12:12, but my career as a bookmaker had now fizzled out, and this no longer applied to me. But I still wanted to continue going to the races, and looked for a new betting angle to remain involved. I knew that turning into a regular punter was unlikely to work; many a figures bookmaker has found it difficult to switch, as it requires such a different approach and attitude. Being a gamekeeper turned poacher (some might call it poacher turned gamekeeper) was not for me.

I came to realise that there might be a future in arbitraging, or 'arbing', between racecourse odds and betting exchange odds, i.e. backing a horse to win on course and to lose on an exchange, and making a tiny profit whatever happened. I was surprised to find that rather than a few opportunities a day, there were sometimes several in a race on different horses, enabling a profit to be made. Margins were very fine and most of the profit went on expenses, which were minimal compared to when I was occupying a pitch; but it was more about the challenge of making it pay and keeping my brain ticking over, as it was necessary constantly to keep one eye on the course prices and the other on the exchange prices, and place bets on both quickly before one or the other market turned against me.

I was also surprised that even some of the strongest bookmakers were reluctant to accept my bets. I used to take lots of business from tic-tacs knowing that another bookmaker was earning from each bet, but if I was offering a price, I wanted to lay it and what anyone was doing with the bet didn't matter. In most areas of business there are wholesalers and retailers, but if manufacturers and wholesalers didn't sell their products to anyone who intended to make a profit from them, how would they ever survive? Gradually on-course markets became less competitive, with fewer bookmakers operating, and trading opportunities became rarer to the point where it is no longer worth even looking for bargains.

I continue to attend meetings of the West of England Bookmakers' Association as a past president, and to go racing, sometimes working for a local bookmaker at racecourses and point-to-points, as a way of remaining in touch with the betting world, but if I am ever asked whether I am thinking of making a comeback, the answer is always a resounding NO. I had never regretted the decision to skip university and follow my vocation, and I never regretted the decision to exit it, though I regretted the reasons that I have explained led to that decision.

Looking through old diaries, racecards and ledgers has prompted many reminiscences about horses, greyhounds, bookmakers and other racecourse characters of my time. Pride of place among horses has to be Arkle, with his contemporary Mill House not far behind. Mill House's reputation suffered from two factors: he was a contemporary of the great Arkle who overshadowed his considerable ability, and he had frequent problems with his back. It was delightful to see him win the Whitbread Gold Cup as top weight in 1967.

In 1973 I watched the Grand National at Towcester instead of going to Aintree. Following the selfish failure of previous owner Lord Sefton to secure Aintree's future after his lifetime, the course had fallen into the hands of property developer Bill Davies, who was threatening to redevelop it and was meanwhile charging extortionate admission charges, so I felt it was every racegoers' duty not to support him. It was a remarkable race in which Australian import Crisp was top weight and made all the running until caught near the winning post by Red Rum. Whenever I see the replay of the run-in, I marvel

Looking back

at how Crisp, though out on his feet, makes a gallant but fruitless attempt to accelerate when Red Rum draws level.

A few years later when John McCririck and I were at a coursing meeting at Altcar, we took the opportunity to visit Ginger McCain's stables in nearby Southport and visit Red Rum in his stable. It was a big stable, but he was a big horse and I was a bit nervous being so close to four potentially lethal legs. But all John could say was that he was hoping Red Rum would lash out and kill me, because 'Red Rum kills rails bookmaker' would be such a scoop!

Another particularly memorable Grand National winner was Rough Quest in 1996. Johanna Williams, who I had collaborated with in creating the Easy-Entry system for trainers, was now the partner of his trainer Terry Casey, and I was delighted to see the horse win for them; although he was 7/1 favourite I had not gone out of my way to lay him, so the occasion was not spoilt by the usual losing Grand National disaster. The following day, I and my own partner Jackie Farrell went by train to Dorking for the traditional National winner's celebration at the stables and I was surprised to find that I could get so much pleasure from someone else's win.

In the months leading up to the 1983 Cheltenham Gold Cup a popular bet offered by the multiple bookmakers had been 20/1 against Michael Dickinson training the first three; I thought at the time, what mugs people must be to take that price – surely one of the other horses at the forefront of the betting will at least get a place. So when the race came and the first five home were all Dickinson trained, it was a timely reminder that I should continue not to let opinion guide my betting.

On the Flat, I saw Nijinsky become the most recent Triple Crown winner at Doncaster in 1970. I recall being impressed when seeing Warning win at Ascot, finishing clear with muscles rippling on his sunlit dark brown body, and ill-fated Shergar was an exceptional Derby winner by a record ten-lengths.

From Bicycle to Bentley, A Bookmaker's Story

The best Waterloo Cup winner I saw was Linden Eland in 1972. I was present at a trial near Huntingdon shortly before when he was put in slips with one of the then favourites for that year's Cup and was most impressive when leading by three lengths; the year after his triumph he had the misfortune to break a leg in the snow in his first round. The best dog I saw at Clonmel was Master Myles, a huge dog who won the Derby there, was unbeaten in twenty-one courses in 1978, and said to have been sold for £30,000, but died in a training accident soon after.

Bookmakers I recall are Archie Scott, probably the only Old Etonian racecourse bookmaker ever; John Joyce, who I remember chatting to singer Bing Crosby at Doncaster; Ru King, a top Midlands bookmaker who was an old man by the time I saw him betting; Duggie Wilson, a frequent protagonist when I was betting on photo-finishes, and who died at Goodwood races, coincidentally on the same pitch where two other bookmakers died during a meeting; and Ted Sturman (Fred Binns), who had a stentorian voice to call the odds.

When I was betting Leslie Steele was one of the strongest of many strong layers in the north. I first met him in the 1960s when I had been in the Silver Ring at Lincoln and there was an objection in the last race. I had watched the finish from behind, and when I wandered into Tatts I saw that Leslie was offering 10/1 against the second, which I thought was good value for my 2/- (10p). The winner was duly disqualified and I collected from him the next day.

A near neighbour on the rails was flamboyant John Banks, who produced an occasional news sheet mocking other racecourse characters; for instance, he wrote that Manchester bookmaker Gus Demmy went into a restaurant and asked 'Do you serve crabs'? and got the reply, 'Sit down sir, we serve anyone'. I was not amused when the story of John's association with jockey John Francome was on the BBC main news and I was included in the footage shown.

When pitch auctions started, Scotsman Freddie Williams achieved his ambition to bet at Cheltenham by buying pick two in Tattersalls.

Looking back

He soon made a name for himself as 'Fearless Freddie', but although he was an experienced bookmaker at horse and greyhound tracks in Scotland, I am not sure that his bookmaking in later life was very professional. Unlike me, he had another business, selling water, which along with running football pools is one of the best money-making wheezes.

Another bookmaker I recall was Josh Newman, who bet next to me at some southern courses. He was not a prominent bookmaker; his main trade was as a furrier, and he would often wear a fur coat when on the rails, which I envied. One quiet day at Kempton, there was a favourite that was 6/4 on every board, when Josh called out 'Who wants 13/8?' Suddenly the ring sprung to life, punters appeared from everywhere and he was stampeded – '£650-400, £260-160 Josh, £325-200, Josh, Josh, have I got my bet, Josh?...', and so on. He immediately realised that he had made a rick and bluffed everyone, saying 'I didn't offer 13/8, I was just asking who wanted it'!

Among the bookmakers I worked for in my early days were Avalon Turf (Eddie Baxter), Frank Bassett (Woofie Goldstein), Dick Best, Ted Blake (A Rawlinson), Frank Butler, Cliff (David Bond), Jim Davies (Jim Arbuckle), Vic Gardner, Peter Graham (Robin Wain), Bernard Howard, Charles James (Charles Woolgar), Tom James (Geraghty), Ladbrokes, Joe Large, Keith Marsden, Lulu Mendoza, Eric Oliver, Mick Redfern, William Reagan (Teddy Bell), Bert Smoothy, John Turner and Noel Wray. Other bookmakers I looked up to as strong layers were Jack Edwards in the West Country, Victor Chandler, Bob Stock (Jim Styles) and later Ron Bolton (Ron Hines) in the South East, Arthur Phillips and Graham Green (Walters & Williams) from Birmingham, Ben Parker and Jack Cowan in the East Midlands, Laurie Wallis, originally from Lincoln, John Hudson from Hull, Harold Greenhalgh from Manchester, Billy Flintham in Yorkshire, Tommy Morton in Scotland, and Terry Rogers and Sean Graham in Ireland.

From Bicycle to Bentley, A Bookmaker's Story

In the 1960s tipsters were a common sight on racecourses. I often saw Prince Monolulu in his colourful exotic garb and headwear, with his catchphrase 'I gotta horse to beat the favourite'. He wasn't a real prince, but came from much humbler origins in the Caribbean. Other tipsters often laid out large photographs of themselves walking with well-known winners and trainers in an attempt to demonstrate their connections and inside knowledge, and would give a long entertaining spiel about the reliability of their tips before trying to sell them in sealed envelopes to the surrounding crowd. Other changes since I started going racing in the 1960s were the advent of starting stalls and overnight declarations, female jockeys and trainers, the installation of the photo-finish at all racecourses and the dying of the art of the tic-tacs; whenever I told someone I worked on the racecourse, the first question was nearly always 'Do I use the tic-tac?'.

Whenever I get asked whether I miss being on the rails, I answer that I certainly don't miss all the travelling, nor the cold and wet weather. At least I can still go racing, whereas I can no longer go coursing in England, which I do miss greatly. I used to regret that I was born too late to catch the best years for racecourse bookmaking, but now I am grateful that the damage wrought by the NJPC came towards the end of my career and not in the middle. Before that I would wonder whether, once the Bentley has gone (given in part exchange after nearly thirty years for my wife's car) and I was back on the bike, people would remember that I started on a bike or just that I used to drive a Bentley! In spite of the challenging hills in Bath, especially up to the racecourse, I have not regressed to an electric bike, as that would be an admission of getting old, one that I am not yet ready to make.

One of the intriguing facets of both racing and coursing has been the wide variety of the people I have encountered, from aristocracy, captains of industry, stars from the world of entertainment, down to the humblest, many of whom were and are the salt of the earth. I have never regretted not going to university, nor the decision to follow the career path I did. When I was still at school my housemaster Peter Lloyd thought I was making a big mistake, but he told me years later when I was back at a school reunion that he often cited me as an example of someone pursuing their dream successfully.

Before Alex Scott became a trainer in Newmarket, his family wanted him to follow a more conventional career, and his mother, Lady Scott, asked me whether they should let him follow his own choice. I don't imagine that I was the sole influence, but drawing on my own experience I said that he should be encouraged to do what he would most enjoy. Alas it did not work out so well for him, as he was shot by a disgruntled employee.

Writing this book has been a bit like living my life over again. I enjoyed it first time round and have enjoyed reliving it all, and I hope you have liked reading it as much as I have liked writing it.

Coursing Appendix

The Waterloo Cup had first been run in 1836 for eight greyhounds, and was instituted by hotelier William Lynn, who named the event after his hotel in Liverpool. Among his many interests he had already leased land from Lord Sefton to open Aintree racecourse, where in 1839, in between days of the Waterloo meeting, he staged a day's racing that included the first incarnation of the Grand National. The Waterloo Cup soon evolved into the Derby of coursing, for 64 of the best dogs from all over Britain and Ireland, and it was many years before it ceased to overshadow the Grand National both as a betting medium and a national sporting event. Sometimes the prize money for the winning owner was more than that for the Epsom Derby, but while those days were in the past, it was still a big sporting occasion. In earlier days, tens of thousands of spectators would attend, with substantial sums being wagered and every club and office having a sweepstake on it, just as on the Derby or Grand National now.

The dogs would run two in each course on a knockout basis over three days in a red or white collar, released by a special lead that consisted of two collars each with a pin mechanism that were released simultaneously by a cord held by the slipper when the dogs pulled away. They were then judged by a red-coated judge on horseback who awarded points on a prescribed scale for speed and agility and signalled the winner with a handkerchief of the appropriate colour. There were consolation stakes, the Waterloo Purse and Waterloo Plate, for first- and second-round losers. Betting took place both on the

Coursing Appendix

individual courses (known as short odds betting) and on the eventual winner (long odds betting). Each year a link of silver, engraved with the year and the name of the winning greyhound, was added to the Waterloo Chain, which was thus one of the most distinctive, and heaviest, trophies of any sport.

It was held in February on Lord Sefton's land at Altcar, near Southport, on peaty turf that had not been ploughed for decades. The public were not allowed onto the field until Lord Sefton arrived, so the surrounding roads and lanes were full of queuing cars and dog vans until he came. He had been trying for many years to win the Cup, and my first year as a bookmaker there was the year that he finally did it with So Clever.

When I first went to the Cup, results were sent to London for onward transmission by one of the same teams from Extel who covered horse racing; every three courses a lad would cycle to a nearby house to phone through the up-to-date results. This was a step up from the days when results were conveyed to London by pigeon post, but in contrast, not many years later bookmaker Norman Mander came to Altcar with a satellite dish that enabled him to show live racing from Hong Kong. Such is the march of technological progress!

There were 64 permanent nominators who had the right to run their own greyhounds; they were all prominent coursing men and women who, as they died or dropped out of coursing, were replaced by election of the Waterloo Committee. If they didn't have a suitable dog fit to run, they would return their nomination to be allocated to any other owner who had applied to run their dogs; such nominations would be filled from among those dogs, selected on merit by the Waterloo Committee. Many years later in 1993 I became a nominator myself, and I sponsored the Cup for several years in the 1990s.

After becoming a Waterloo nominator I owned some dogs in partnership with Sally Merison, who ran the Alresford Coursing Club and was chairman of the National Coursing Club. In the 1998 Waterloo Cup we ran Winning Master, who was joint 10-1 favourite;

I was not optimistic, as I thought that, though he had speed, he wouldn't be tough enough to see out the six rounds required to win. After easily winning his first course, he was unsighted (i.e. lost sight of the hare) in the second round, so didn't even stay in contention long enough to prove me right. We fared better in 2000 with Fenian, who was narrowly beaten in his first round by one of the shortest long odds favourites for many years and went on to be beaten in the final of the Purse consolation stake. Better still to come was Marks Legacy, named as a tease to Sally's son Mark. In 2002 she lost the final of the Purse, and the following year she won the Purse outright.

The sport of coursing is an ancient one and has been mentioned by Roman writers, not as a means of hunting game to eat but as a sport to test the agility of greyhounds, as now. The rules that governed modern coursing, including the points awarded for various turns, etc., date from Tudor times, when no one below the rank of nobility was allowed to own a greyhound. In 1776 the Swaffham Coursing Club was formed, and the system of coursing clubs all over the country organising coursing meetings in open countryside on local farmland evolved from then.

The spread of railways throughout the country enabled the public to attend meetings, thus popularising the sport. Although open coursing was always the predominant form in Britain, there was a brief period in the late nineteenth century when enclosed, or park, coursing was popular, including at racecourses such as Gosforth Park at Newcastle, Kempton Park and Plumpton. This is the variety of coursing – in a prepared field with an escape that hares can use but dogs cannot – most common in Ireland, where open coursing is rare.

Both forms are tests of stamina, as dogs have to be able to run a number of rounds at a meeting, depending on whether a stake is for 4, 8, 16, 32 or 64 dogs – there have even been 128-dog stakes – but whereas open coursing tests both speed and agility, in park coursing all the emphasis is on speed, with the hare often through the escape before the dogs get near it. In park coursing the length of time the dogs run tends to be fairly consistent, but in open coursing it can be very variable, depending on whether the hare goes through a hedge early on or disappears over the horizon with the dogs several fields away. This can make a big difference, referred to as the handicap, in the next round if a dog that has had a short course of twenty seconds meets one that has a course of more than a minute. Whereas coursing dogs would sometimes be required to run up to three times in a day, present-day greyhound racing has a rule that prevents dogs running more than once in four days. I believe that in time this will result in the greyhound breed becoming softer and less sound, just as many racehorse trainers have said that the obsession with watering courses will have a similar effect on the thoroughbred breed.

Once at Huntingdon the course disappeared out of sight with the judge following, so the crowd knew it must be a long course and waited for the judge to reappear to gauge some idea of how long the course had been. As the seconds and minutes ticked by, we all thought what a marathon course it must have been, but it transpired when the judge returned that he had got off his horse near a wood to relieve himself!

The coursing that I followed was for greyhounds, which had to be registered in a recognised greyhound stud book, and was by far the most common form of organised coursing under rules, but there were sometimes meetings for other breeds of sight hounds, or gazehounds, such as deerhounds, wolfhounds, salukis and whippets, which were all much slower. I do recall when being at a coursing meeting at Huntingdon seeing a whippet coursing meeting in the distance several fields away.

The practice of trespassing on a farm without the landowner's permission and setting dogs on a hare is sometimes described as coursing, but is more properly described as poaching. It still takes place sometimes, regrettably, but it has always been illegal, even before the Hunting Act banned organised coursing, when it was resented by followers of coursing as it gave us all a bad name and deterred landowners from tolerating hares to facilitate meetings, instead of culling them to protect their crops.

Since time immemorial, there have been antis who wanted to see hunting and coursing banned. Some changed their minds when they came to see the sport for themselves and realised that the propaganda they had been fed was not in line with reality, but most were too biased even to believe their own eyes. I recall one TV debate in the early 1970s when those against coursing refused to believe that you could find hares just by walking through a field – they must have thought they all lived in apartment blocks somewhere, and that when they got old, they went to old hares' homes to spend their last days. One anti even claimed that it would be better for the entire species of hares to be wiped out than for coursing to continue – surely not a view that any hare would agree with.

Eventually the antis got their way – first in Scotland, where hunting and coursing were made illegal in 2002, leading to the demise of the only Scottish coursing club still running under NCC rules, the Scottish National Club. England and Wales followed in 2005 after debates in both Houses of Parliament occupying several hundred hours of valuable parliamentary time and the last Waterloo Cup was held in February of that year. I was in the public gallery of the House of Lords during one of the many debates on the Hunting Bill, when the minister in charge of the Bill, Alun Michael, quoted some numbers of hares killed in various activities. He said that each year around 200,000 hares were killed in hare shoots, so that's alright to continue; around 1,600 hares are killed when hunted by beagles and harriers, so perhaps that should be banned; and about 200 hares are killed at coursing meetings, so that must be banned. Topsy-turvy thinking or what?

Prime Minister Tony Blair thought the Hunting Bill important enough to attend the Commons to vote in its favour, but when the issue was whether to send British troops to war in Iraq, he didn't attend to vote on that. He later admitted that the passing of the Hunting

Bill was the biggest mistake of his premiership – any impartial hare would agree, as hares were shot in their thousands on land where farmers previously tolerated them. It had long been recognised that the best places to find hares were where coursing took place.

The more extreme antis would like to see the keeping of pets and eating meat banned, but meanwhile the next targets seem to be greyhound racing and pigeon racing, followed no doubt by horse racing and any other sport or activity involving animals. They would be bereft if they ever found there was nothing to protest about, but I expect they would manage to find something.

Mention of pigeon racing reminds me of when I witnessed the start of a pigeon race on a disused airfield near Bath. A lorry arrived carrying hundreds of homing pigeons in individual cages on each side with a mechanism designed to open them all simultaneously. When the driver pulled the lever at the appointed time, most of the birds flew out to the left and right of the lorry, literally getting a flier, but some cages remained closed and he had to go round and open those by hand. It made me think that if the stalls on racecourses were like that, with horses starting in different directions and some being released behind the rest, racing would be somewhat chaotic!

To see coursing now I have to go to Ireland, where I tell people I am a political refugee. I had first gone coursing in Ireland in 1969 when I went to the Irish Cup at Clounanna near Limerick, and I first went to the National Coursing Festival on the horse racecourse at Clonmel in 1974, since when I have been a regular there, missing very few years. The Festival consists of the Derby for 64 dog puppies and the Oaks for 64 bitch puppies, and also Champion stakes for 8 older dogs and 8 older bitches. Puppies have to qualify by winning a Trial Stake at one of the many coursing clubs throughout Ireland, and the older dogs by winning stakes during the season. Every Irish courser's ambition is to have a runner, let alone a winner, at Clonmel; following on from Marks Legacy's success at Altcar, she was bred to Derby winner Hilltown, but the puppies we kept from the litter never came near to qualifying for Clonmel. They would have been better suited to English coursing, being more of an all-round test of speed and agility, as they lacked enough of the pure speed required for Irish coursing.

Clonmel is also a major social event where coursing fans from all over Northern and Southern Ireland, and many from Britain and other countries, gather for a few days. When I first went, there was a separate open coursing meeting on the Sunday, the main coursing on Monday, Tuesday and Wednesday, and horseracing on Thursday. Hotels for miles around would be fully booked from year to year; for many years I stayed at the Clonmel Arms in the centre of the town, within walking distance of the course, and occasionally at Hotel Minella, a name familiar to followers of National Hunt racing. Many of the hotels were the scene of all-night poker games, as well as all-night drinking – few attendees wanted to waste time sleeping. The 'Arms' closed around the turn of the century, became a sorry sight with weeds growing from the windows and remains a disused building in poor condition. Now the Festival is just the three main days, including part or all of the weekend, and with the improvement in roads all over Ireland, fewer people stay, but it remains a Mecca for greyhound people from both sides of the Irish Sea, and further afield. I was never a poker player, but there were a few years in the early 1980s when backgammon was very popular at Clonmel, causing me some late nights.

Betting Appendix

Betting odds can be expressed in one of two ways: decimal or fractional. Fractional is the traditional format, such as 3/1 or 13/8, and decimal is the return to one unit, including stake, such as 4.0 or 2.625, just as tote dividends are returned, and simply 1 added to the fractional odds to 1. On the racecourse odds are always displayed as fractions, on exchanges as decimal, and most other betting sites provide a setting to choose your preference. The percentage figure for each rate of odds is derived by dividing 100 by the decimal price or the fractional plus one; thus for 3/1 it is 25%, for 13/8 it is 38.0952%. To put it another way, it is the amount you would have to stake at the price to return exactly £100 including stake.

The mathematical basis of bookmaking is the sum of percentage figure for the odds of each runner in any event; if they add up to more than 100, the figures are described as over-round, and are in the bookmaker's favour, and if they add to less than 100, they are overbroke and favour the punters. Here are two examples from the Cheltenham Festival in 2023:

Champion Hurdle		
	SP	%
Constitution Hill	4/11	73.33
State Man	7/2	22.22
Vauban	16/1	5.88
I Like To Move It	25/1	3.85
Zanahir	66/1	1.49
Not So Sleepy	150/1	0.66
Jason The Militant	250/1	0.40
		107.84

Gold Cup		
	SP	%
Galopin Des Champs	7/5	41.67
A Plus Tard	4/1	20.00
Bravemansgame	6/1	14.29
Ahoy Senor	14/1	6.67
Noble Yeats	14/1	6.67
Stattler	16/1	5.88
Minella Indo	20/1	4.76
Conflated	22/1	4.35
Protektorat	25/1	3.85
Hewick	40/1	2.44
Royale Pagaille	50/1	1.96
Sounds Russian	50/1	1.96
Eldorado Allen	100/1	0.99
		115.47

Charles Dickens' Mr Micawber might have said 101%, result happiness, 99%, result misery, but it is not as simple as that. If the percentages add up to more than 100%, that proves only that some of the runners are under the true odds, not that they all are; a bookmaker who offers 4/6 heads and 11/10 tails might think he is betting well, with the figures in his favour, but he won't make it pay over time. To ensure the theoretical profit, it is necessary to lay all the horses in exactly the right proportions, which in practice is virtually impossible, and while the over-rounds in the examples above are 7.84 and 15.47, the margins in the layer's favour are not 7.84% and 15.47% but 7.84/107.84, which is 7.27%, and 15.47/115.47, which is 13.40%. It is of course the prices in the book that count, rather than those on the board or on paper, and generally the steamers steam because they have been laid at higher prices and the drifters drift because they have not been laid at the lower prices.

However the higher the over-round, the more likely the layer is to profit over time, and the easier it should be to achieve a book with no, or few, losers, especially with the hedging facility provided by betting exchanges.

Betting Appendix

When calculating the margin for place betting, the total of the percentages for the place prices, which are the relevant fraction of the win price, has to be compared not with 100 but 100 times the number of places involved. The standard fractions of ¼ or ⅕ win odds usually produce place betting with a viable percentage, but can throw up anomalies when there is a very short-priced favourite. Rules for racecourse bookmakers do not permit the use of smaller fractions in this circumstance, so the result is that bookmakers who bet each way have to offer second and third favourites at much shorter odds than those who are betting win only.

It seems that it has not occurred to the rulemakers that punters might prefer to have, say, £10 each way at 7/1, ⅙ odds a place rather than at 5/1, ⅕ odds a place. When starting prices were formed from the racecourse market, the system was set to ignore any win-only layers, even though the definition of SP was supposed to be a report of the best prices available to reasonable amounts at the course; this was a distortion of the truth of which Josef Goebbels would have been proud.

When the Covid pandemic prevented racegoers from attending courses, SPs were necessarily formed from off-course bookmakers, and that did not change when crowds returned. Statistics show that average overrounds are much the same as before, but it has been acknowledged that this is because although the prices of the first few in the betting on each race tend to be shorter, the outsiders are at longer prices than they generally used to be. It is surprising that racecourses and course bookmakers, who pay a so-called marketing fee to courses in addition to their enhanced admission fees, have not seized on this to encourage punters to come racing.

There are punters who don't seem to care about what odds they are getting on their selection, when I see someone take 7/1 when the same horse is 8/1 with the bookmaker either side. And I sometimes wonder whether arithmetic is still taught in schools when I am in the crowd near the rails and someone asks me which is better, 7/2 or 4/1. It is so tempting just to answer that I always preferred 7/2.

Clerking before computers

Below is an extract from my ledger for a race at Taunton in December 1998, showing how bets are recorded in such a way as to show the current state of the book being made, i.e. potential profit or loss. Under each horse's name are five columns: from left to right they contain the running total of the potential take-out, or pay-out on that horse, the winnings and stake, the running total of all stakes on the race, and the ticket number or name of the punter, with a ring round it if the stake is not paid on and a T if it is a trade telephone bet. The place part of an each way bet is marked with a ring, and a back, or hedging, bet is shown with a ring around the whole five columns, with the bet being subtracted from the running total. The bookmaker can thus see his liabilities just by comparing the take-out for each horse with the total stakes. The hyphen after a figure denotes 50p, a small cross 75p and a dash 25p. After the race the winning ticket numbers and the back bets are crossed off as they are paid.

Clerking before computers

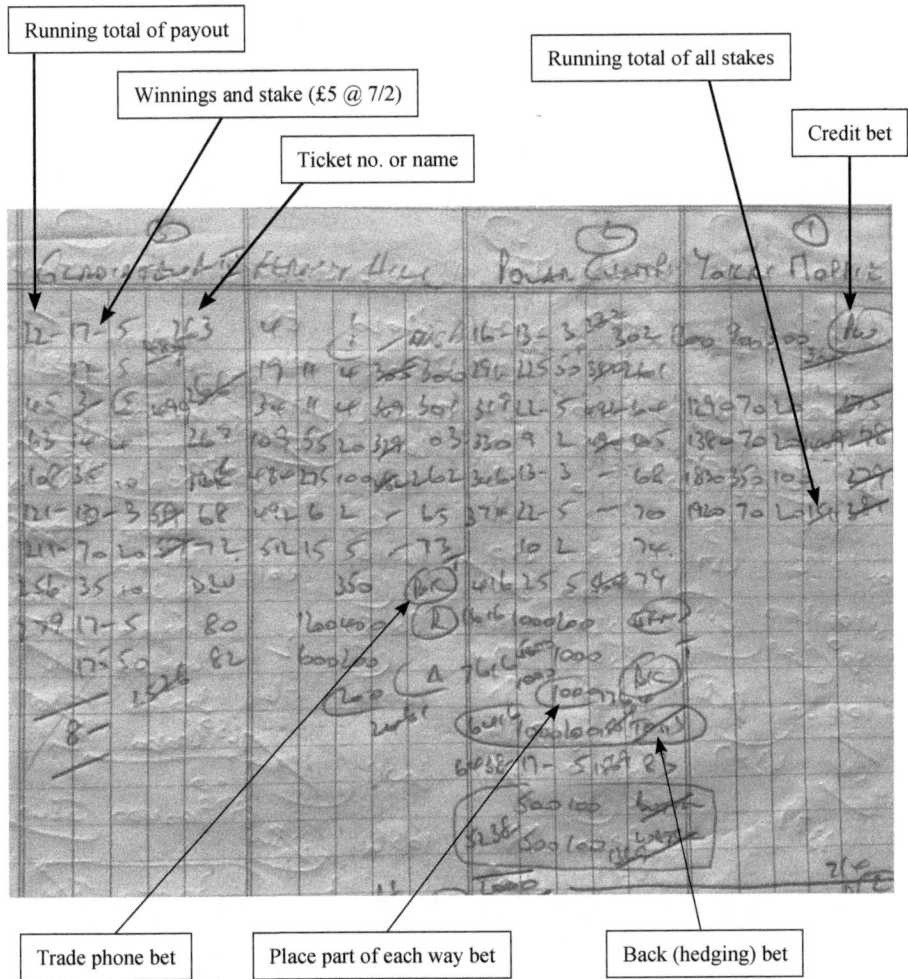

The ledger would be printed with eight or ten columns on each page. There were also ledgers designed more for rails bookmakers with a wider column for names and two extra columns for place bets. These had only six columns per page, which is nearer to the number of horses often laid in a race.